WHY CONSERVATISM HAS BECOME ANTI-CONSERVATION

The Science and Politics of an Environmental Maladaptation

Alex F. Lechich

CARL WOESE (1928–2012) developed the modern gene sequence-based understanding of biological organization, showing that evolutionary lineages can be tracked to a common ancestral state.

That clashed with the prevailing scientific wisdom and when asked how he felt about it said:

"I point to the moon and they focus on my finger."

This acknowledgment goes out to my brother Roy, English bard and musician extraordinaire, and giver of good writing advice including reining in wanderings that go a bit far afield and other sound wisdom, and for our discourses over the years on politics, life and liberty (and sailing), that provided not only a sounding board for refinement of thought but also a worldview in fine tune with today's humanity (upon which were issued occasional rays of hope that salved his brother's somewhat more chary and cynical outlook).

TABLE OF CONTENTS

INTRODUCTION

As a retired federal environmental (marine) scientist, I have had a front-row seat on how environmental laws and regulations have been developed and implemented in this country over the last thirty or so years. During that time, and even more so in the fifteen years earlier (beginning in the late 1960's) some truly groundbreaking environmental laws were written and implemented, and huge improvements in our air and water have resulted. That level or rate of improvement has not continued though, and regarding climate change in particular, very little has happened toward better management of man's industry that impacts the environment. I felt that there were some very specific reasons that could be largely responsible for this poor recent record, and for the present situation where it seems our ability to implement additional needed regulatory reforms for the environment in general and for climate change has effectively been halted. It probably wouldn't surprise many people if, coming from a fairly liberal environmental scientist, at least one cause for this lack of movement is suggested to be the actions of conservative politicians in concert with industry that tend to block stricter environmental regulation. In my experience it's a fairly commonly held opinion in the environmental field that this relationship exists, but it is mainly considered as kind of a background issue and just a fact of life. That conservatives generally lean against environmental reforms is also probably a fairly widely-held perception in the general population, though perhaps in a somewhat vague sense and not necessarily considered as an overriding concern. After all, there have always been political divides in our society and they are considered to be a normal aspect of our democratic system. I thought, though, that perhaps this political factor of conservatism in environmental decision-making is more of an issue than might be commonly believed. So, it seemed to me that taking a closer look at the phenomenon might be a useful contribution.

The first purpose would be to get a better understanding of how critical an issue political obstructionism by conservatives actually is in the implementation of improved environmental regulation. The other goal (based partly on the findings of the first) was to better understand the origins, motivations and boundaries of conservatism regarding its likelihood of continuing to limit regulatory improvements, especially in this time of seriously degrading environmental conditions.

The deeper I looked into first the history and then the relevant science and psychological factors of conservatism's stance against environmental reforms, the more I felt this could in fact be the most important, in fact overriding, factor in implementing better environmental regulation. The fact that it is at least a significant factor is quite easily demonstrated by looking even briefly at the legislative history of environmental regulation, which is done in the first chapter. This book then lays out the main case that resulted from my investigation in what is obviously a quite controversial area. Starting with the assumption that the inability to substantially improve environmental regulation would result in continuing degradation of the environment (what has been in place till now has too often not worked very well), the effort then was to evaluate why a significant segment of the population would act in seemingly self destructive ways from an evolutionary standpoint. (Obviously, any species, including man, that is unable to maintain adequately healthy living conditions for itself is not looking at very good odds for long term survival, or at the very least for prospering.)

After examining the possible mechanisms for how and why conservatism would include such apparently self-destructive and illogical behaviors (and summarizing drastically), the conclusion reached is that our two main political value systems evolved directly from our two primal behavioral mechanisms (described in detail later as conservatism having evolved from our competitive drives, liberalism from those associated with cooperation). Since these behavioral systems are genetically ingrained, those individuals who present a robust version of either of these will bind tightly with the particular views associated in each. And because of the hardwired nature of these behaviors, the particular views can persist even in the face of fairly clear and convincing evidence to the contrary. So, since conservatives will tend to block environmental reforms (as will be demonstrated), and they maintain a sizable, though not overwhelming, proportion in the population and political representation, it's very likely they will continue to block urgently needed environmental legislation (as will be also described, liberals are not an issue here). It seems that only if a much broader and stronger environmental movement takes hold can this trend be turned around. Such a movement might perhaps be strengthened if it included a new, broad recognition that this political value system (conservatism) has essentially become a maladaptive mindset that is consistently opposed to improved environment reforms.

My career in government environmental agencies was a mostly enjoyable one, especially when it included being out on the water, which was luckily the case in several of those positions. Being involved in and observing how environmental regulations are made and implemented was also interesting. One aspect in the making of environmental laws and regulations that was evident in the various areas I was involved in was the presence of a fairly consistent set of opponents. When there were any political aspects to the project or permit (which was often), it was typically environmentalists and mainly liberal politicians on one side, and industry and its supporters, mainly conservative politicians, on the other.

The industry side has of course always pressed for more lenient regulatory requirements, and its influence has usually been effective at least to some degree. This is probably because it has used the reasonable-sounding arguments of economic costs, which resonate with a large part of the population and with politicians (we will set aside for now other costs, social and environmental, that are not yet very effectively considered in environmental regulation). In the areas associated with water concerns, either fresh or salt, that I've mostly been involved with, the two forces seemed to be somewhat counterbalanced, perhaps because of the strong emotional connections ordinary people feel about "their" water and ocean. However, on the issue of climate change one can easily see how the balance has shifted to the industry side, at least in this country. The grouping of industry and its supporters has been quite vocal and politically powerful enough to suppress the more restrictive regulations proposed in international settings, mainly through "no" votes by conservatives in the US Senate. In addition, the economic pressures now present in the United

States are seemingly beginning to diminish the available funding and efforts in other areas of environmental regulation, including for protecting the air, waters, wetlands, and the development of pollution control technologies and practices in general.

This book is not intended to be another study of global climate change or a review of other environmental conditions, including the ongoing pollution of our air and waters. Those areas have been extensively studied and reported by experts in the relevant fields, and anyone interested in them can find numerous sources. There will also be no attempt to try to convince readers of the reality of man-made global climate change, or of the fairly dire environmental degradation of our air, oceans, and other waters in many parts of the world that was caused by man. Regarding climate change, readers who have already chosen to not believe the vast body of expert scientists in the field will probably find themselves somewhat left behind in this discussion. As far as I'm concerned, that train has left the station, and I'm not interested in trying to convince people who have made their decision on man-made climate change based on factors other than real science. As indicated above, I am not a climate scientist, nor have I looked with any detail at climate data, since it is not an area of particular interest for me. I've found no reason to disbelieve the almost universal consensus of climatologists who have generated and studied the data and made their conclusions. Why would I (or any reasonable, unbiased person, in my opinion) put a lot of effort into questioning their findings? They are, for me anyway, fellow scientists who are bound by the same scientific method and principles as are the scientists in my field and in all other scientific disciplines. Should I have to become immersed in the field in which they are experts and in many cases have devoted their entire careers and often lives to, just to prove to myself that they are correct? Of course, the only reason to even ask that question is that there are groups, mainly those associated with industries of various kinds and the conservatives who are of like views and often backed by them, who have in fact decided that most climate scientists and those who support them are lying.

It's interesting how some of these folks seem to choose what branch of science to believe in. If it is a science that is irrefutable by obvious proof, such as aspects of nuclear physics that have been demonstrated partly by Hiroshima and Nagasaki, or areas in biology that have come up with life-saving medicines, they kind of have to go along with it. If the science does not challenge their belief systems, they are typically fine with whatever they understand of it. But if it proffers any challenge to their belief systems—like evolution for religionists or climate science for free marketers and libertarians—suddenly they either become instant scientific experts themselves or they become faithful devotees of the few remaining "other scientists" who still hold opposing views. These "other scientists," in the case of climate change, are almost invariably either paid for by an energy or industry group, are wannabes for that privilege, or are outright quacks.

Most people wouldn't think they'd have to immerse themselves in a scientific field before allowing themselves to believe what the experts in it have found, no more than those who would think they'd have to study medicine before believing the diagnosis of their doctors. This is actually a good analogy since, even for people who get a second or third medical opinion, they will at some point act to go with the prevailing opinion. In the case of climate science, the opinion among climate scientists is so overwhelmingly consistent that, applying the medical analogy, anyone with a serious illness searching for a contrary opinion before acting would probably have been long since dead. Those who are shackled by religious or conservative convictions such as to overwhelm their ability to objectively evaluate scientific arguments will probably not be here long. Having preconceived notions of the conservative kind makes it difficult (as we'll see) for individuals to be open to alternative views, even when supported with logical arguments. Those brave enough to try, though, are of course welcome. You may find it interesting, and, in the best of all worlds, might even be convinced to come on over to the light side.

I've had long involvement with the political aspects of how environmental regulation is developed and implemented. While with the US Environmental Protection Agency (EPA) in New York City, I worked with its headquarters in Washington, DC on updating the US ocean-dumping regulations, a politically-charged topic in many areas of the country. The main issue in ocean dumping these days is the disposal of dredged material from harbors and channels (in contradiction to an apparently common misperception household garbage disposal in the ocean has been outlawed for many years, and the last few remaining chemical and sewage sludge ocean dumping operations were halted in the 1980's in the US). Environmental groups and the shipping industry have been the major stakeholders in this political battle. The updated regulations and more sensitive testing regimes associated with them were eventually applied in the dredging of the Port of New York and New Jersey (which was-shameless plug here-the subject of my first book, *A Storm in the Port: Keeping the Port of New York and New Jersey Open*.) I later worked for New York State's Department of Environmental Conservation (NYSDEC) in its marine program, and with its headquarters in Albany in updating and implementing the state's dredging regulations. In between those positions (and after owning and operating a restaurant on the Jersey shore) I worked for a NJ Township water utility. Seeing government and the public stakeholders in action on environmental regulation at the federal, state and municipal levels were eye-opening experiences. There were the expected positions from industry groups at those different levels, though with some nuances, and there were some surprises from environmental groups that I wrote about in the dredging book. The main surprise was that environmental groups sometimes shoot themselves in the foot by, idiosyncratic as it may sound, aiming too high. By this I mean sometimes (though rarely) making claims of potential environmental harm that go beyond what is scientifically indicated. What that does, in my opinion, is make them an easy target for industry boosters, who use any such mistakes to scoff them and their efforts, and diminish the real and serious issues that they mainly raise. Of course, the anti-environmentalists have raised invalid points and shot out spurious claims on a constant and on-going basis, but it seems important that the good guys keep themselves aligned on a higher plane. Accurate assessment of the actual potential harm is therefore I think crucial in proposing and implementing any environmental regulation. Fairness, and in the end, credibility, requires that positions be taken carefully and with scientific justification. This book has strived to do that in terms of the science cited and applied, and the logical interpretations that were made with any of the information that was used, to the best extent possible.

I often wondered, working in environmental science with also an early interest in economics (after a stint in the US Army, I went back to college as an economics major, very briefly) and politics, why some people seem to be almost oblivious to environmental issues compared with others who seem to care more about them. I had found it almost inconceivable that there are people that have apparently little concern for the possible effects of their actions or those of others on the environment, when not only themselves but their children or grandchildren can suffer the consequences. I once watched an old man in a southern coastal state throw right into the bay all the paper and plastic packaging for some crab bait that he was using with traps deployed off the dock. He committed the act in the presence of two youngsters, who were apparently his grandchildren. It can be understood how some people can act this way, out of the manner of their upbringing, ignorance, and sloth, with the above incident probably an example of all three. (Hopefully, those kids learned differently from their school and modern societal views). This kind of littering pollution is a generally low level type of polluting behavior, and it is probably driven mainly by sloth and ignorance. Greed is usually the main driver for more serious polluters. Most low level polluting behaviors are more likely to occur under the rationalization that perhaps not much harm would ensue after all (most people would like to believe their actions are not causing much harm), and both kinds of polluting behavior are more likely when there is a good chance of escaping detection or consequences.

So it is left to government mainly the role of regulating public and private activities that can result in pollution and other adverse environmental effects that all of us must bear in the long run. (To those conservatives who are still here and feel that industry should be left to regulate itself under the inherent restraints of capitalism, all I can say is, they've had plenty of chance to do so.) The role that Congress plays in environmental regulation is obviously a key one. More will be discussed about Congress later in the book; leave it here to say I think that most of our politicians, from left to right and in between, are largely bought and paid for by the moneyed interests in this country, mainly the large industrial and financial corporations. Going by the dead low opinion-poll numbers for Congress these days it seems that many Americans share this or a similar view. These unholy alliances are a huge part of the problems facing this country regarding environmental degradation generally as well as, by our remaining great influence abroad, global climate change. Of course, saying that many of both left and right-wing politicians are corrupted might seem at odds with the case made earlier, that it is the actions of conservatives that tend to block stronger environmental laws. But it should be remembered that the key point is the strong natural and psychological linkage of industry mainly with those of a conservative bent, and the actions that this relationship most often leads to. And as will be further discussed later, the big environmental decisions and votes almost always go along political party (but mainly liberal-conservative) lines. To be fair, it isn't always just conservative politicians who vote against environmental reform. When liberal or moderate politicians vote against stronger environmental laws for reasons mainly to do with political contributions, it's an even worse offense in my book. At least the conservatives can be thought of as going along with their principles (as wrong as they might be, and to what degree other factors might also be at play), while proclaimed liberals or moderates that vote against the environment to mainly appease the interests of wealthy and powerful contributors (regardless of whatever other excuse they might try to come up with) are beyond contemptible.

There is also in later parts of the book a discussion of certain economic and financial issues that can relate very strongly to the implementation of environmental reforms. Here, a faction of current conservative philosophy is granted as being the correct view in the author's opinion. This is in relation to the government policies and actions associated with the current US Federal Reserve banking system.

The investigation into the questions above required crossing over into various other scientific fields. This is not something done lightly by any scientist, as it is fraught with pitfalls having to do with the restrictions in the scientific method and with protectionism within the disciplinary fiefdoms. The scientific method typically requires setting narrow hypotheses and objectives and that usually entails restricting an investigation to one scientific discipline (some exceptions might include where certain testing methods or other technologies are necessary parts of an experiment). The protectionism aspect is a significant obstacle as well and will be further discussed below. Regardless of these pitfalls, I knew that there was no one looking into or even talking much about this situation in the field of environmental science that I was aware of (except maybe in hushed tones around the water cooler), nor would it be likely addressed in any other science field, for the reasons given above.

Some might ask, what is the point in going through all this? Even if the case is made here quite solidly that conservatives generally are against environmental reforms (and even though it may already be commonly believed to some degree), what is to be done about it? In a democracy such as the US you can't very well exclude a significant portion of the population from participating in the democratic process, can you? (Actually, as an aside, it obviously has happened in the past and perhaps may still be happening in some degree, as many civil rights advocates insist. Any liberals that might be salivating at the thought of applying it to conservatives any time soon, though, should probably give it up.) What is hoped is that perhaps this book can help to dispel in even a small way the apparently common notion that although conservative ideology may include skepticism about environmental protections, it is a legitimate adversarial political position which must be defended in our democratic form of government. The reality is that modern conservatism actually includes a deeply held, ingrained drive to stifle environmental protections based on some basic and intrinsically held conservative psychological characteristics. This can no longer be considered a healthy political give-and-take, not in the global environmental circumstances we are now in and getting deeper into. We are not in Kansas anymore. The hope is that by demonstrating this phenomenon clearly here it might change some peoples' (realistically, mainly political independents and undecided moderates) views on this issue, and thereby perhaps help to grow a more broad-based political rejection of conservatism's anti-environmental agenda.

Environmental science has made great strides in collecting and processing field data and information and using it for implementing better environmental controls which resulted in vast improvements in our air, water and the reduction of pollution in general. Even my small role in the field as the key EPA staffer during a critical period in the mid 1990's (generally known as the Port of NY/NJ dredging crisis) hopefully resulted in some small improvement in the conditions of our nearby coastal ocean. The port industry was the main opposition in this case, as well as the US Army Corps of Engineers (USACE), mainly because they had not developed alternatives to ocean disposal (not for lack of trying, but nevertheless not in a serious enough and timely fashion), and then had to scramble when the writing was on the wall. After some stimulating rounds of negotiations and serious political heat coming from both sides (including vice-president Al Gore's office and regional port-related industry), EPA finally made the right decision and the entirety of the tighter testing and evaluation regime of the new national guidelines were implemented. (The EPA Regions and Corps Districts have some leeway in how and to what degree to implement these types of nationally-developed guidelines, and the pressure was great on upper management to avoid any touted harm to regional industry. Some important environmental groups were pushing just as strongly the other way, and when upper management feels conflicted and stressed, the pain tends to flow downhill. Thereafter your humble author left EPA to own and operate a restaurant on the Jersey Shore, which, though a quite intriguing experience turned out to be neither much of a respite from stress nor a satisfying vocational change.) Nevertheless, apart from some early environmental gains, the current situation in many parts of the country and the world is fairly dire, especially with respect to global climate change. So really, if one was to think seriously about it, what further real good can be expected from the science if its application in the world is oftentimes effectively stymied by a persistent political oppositional mindset?

This political factor, conservatism's role in blocking environmental reform, is after all outside the science itself but often has an overriding control over whether any of its findings is actually implemented in regulation. How can any environmental scientist or anyone serious about improving the environment ignore it or pretend it doesn't exist? I knew what industry and conservative politicians had accomplished in minimizing or even reversing at times more effective environmental requirements, and it seemed obvious from reading of the events and the accounts of climate scientists that this clearly seemed to be happening in regard to climate-change. Also, I may be biased but when considering the conditions that we now face on this planet, what can possibly be a more important endeavor than trying to help reverse this trend and getting us on a more sustainable environmental footing? What ultimate benefit, after all, will come from achieving just about any other human goal, even the most desired social reform or medical breakthrough, if the environmental conditions for our very survival on this planet become compromised? If that is in fact beginning to happen now (as it clearly is), wouldn't the expenditure of human energy, talent and capital to accomplish any other thing, while ignoring or minimizing the urgent needs of our environment, be kind of a waste?

So I bit the bullet and grew immersed in the fields I thought would be likely to shed light on these questions, including evolution science, neurobiology, genetics, paleoanthropology, and psychology. As a biologist (BS) and a marine environmental scientist (MS), I've had formal training in the first three of the above fields, and I've read fairly extensively in the other two as my investigation brought me to them. After completing the investigation and writing up the results, I had initially intended to have these ideas published in a peer-reviewed journal in a field such as evolution science or social biology (though the underlying subject was of course the environment and its management, the science and discussion in the paper itself was mainly outside of the field), but alas this was not to be. One of the rejections included the specific comments of the three assigned peer reviewers, which I read with extreme interest. All three were un-named, of course, until I later requested and was granted further consultation with one of them. Two of these reviewers had some quite positive comments, and all expressed a high interest in the thesis.

The two more positive reviewers were obviously involved in the field of evolution science (the one I later contacted definitely is), while the third appeared to be in a social science field. The reviewer I later contacted had this initial comment: *"I found this paper interesting and highly original and basically plausible: evolutionary theory as a foundation for political philosophy. I hope the author understands therefore, why I have to recommend rejection (with the option of resubmission after extensive revision): because his message is too important to be presented as-is. I suspect Lechich's main problem is impatience."* The other reviewer, apparently also an evolution scientist, had this to say: *"To address such a large and vexing question in a single scientific paper requires either, (a) an absolute mastery of evolutionary theory (biological and cultural) as well as a very deep understanding of political philosophy, political economy and the policy process, OR (b) simplifying many of the key concepts and theories to such an extent that you lose the real value of the paper. I believe that this paper represents the latter. This is not a knock on the author - very few individuals, if any, could successfully do what this author hoped to accomplish. The sub-questions related to the key question noted above could make up many, many dissertations."*

The second reviewer's comment that simplifying key concepts and theories resulted in losing the real value of the paper speaks volumes about the policies of today's peer-reviewed journals. The commenter seems to be saying that either the paper simplified too much, or essentially it should encompass a large body of the science and knowledge suggested in his first option (how otherwise can an author demonstrate his absolute mastery and deep understanding of it all?) So apparently, simplifying concepts and theories, even if only by means of selecting findings from one or more fields to make a broader, cross-disciplinary point (as the paper sought to do), wouldn't do unless one is an expert in those fields as well. The first option in the comment (total and holistic mastery) would result in such a large body of work that it would obviously not fit for a journal paper. (Perhaps this was the intention of the reviewer, in which case the comment has merit in the regard that I did finally decide to do this book. I wonder, though, if any writer could ever encompass the total mastery and understanding that reviewer seemed to require.) The first reviewer's comment doesn't seem to jibe fundamentally with these views, since he (I know he's a he) leaves room for acceptance upon extensive revision. Of course different reviewers have different opinions, but their differences were such as to disqualify or not the approach entirely. And obviously, I had no desire to write many, many dissertations. More to the point, though, these and other responses seemed to point out the unlikely prospect that any peer-reviewed journal today would publish the paper, no matter how much extensive revision was done or how much absolute mastery of evolutionary theory or psychology was obtained.

Perhaps, as the first reviewer noted, I was impatient. However, as noted above, I didn't see this issue being raised anywhere, and if not now, when? As much as I might respect the scientific competence of both of the above reviewers, their more specific comments (which I won't subject the reader to) each suggested further consideration of completely different aspects of evolution science, and to comply with them both would have required a tome. Though I have in fact done considerable additional research on some of the aspects all the reviewers suggested, and this book reflects that, I resolved to not resubmit the paper to any peer-reviewed journals. There are obviously clear advantages for focusing on specialized knowledge, including the ability to better allocate research effort, peer review, and resources, and thereby for narrowing and specializing scientific fields. This can sometimes stifle creativity, however, when looking at problems that cross over into other disciplines. Perhaps a more interdisciplinary journal that can recognize new thinking, even if in topics that can be politically controversial, is a solution. The huge growth and fairly broad technical acceptance of some open-access scientific journals seem to point to the apparently widely held perception that an alternative to the existing peer-reviewed journals can be desirable. (I have to admit to having less respect for the apparent socio-psychological reviewer's response, since it failed wholly to comprehend a basic distinction stated in the paper between republicans and conservatism. The thesis relates to conservatism, not strictly to the Republican Party's views, so the reviewer's comment that former Governor Schwarzenegger might not fall into those precepts totally missed the point, since he is generally not conservative on these issues.) In any case I decided my research and conclusions would be better presented in the form of a book.

Not only would this permit a fuller treatment of more aspects of the subject, but it would also let me make it more accessible and interesting reading for the general public. (Of course, I later found similar restrictions with the established book publishers. In looking at the manuscript as being either science or politics, the potential science publishers shied from the political aspects and the more edgy political publishers seemed uncomfortable with the amount of science. This partly led to my going with assisted self-publication.)

The arguments made against the original paper, and probably many more, will be made against the book. I would request and advise potential critics, though, since a book is a more public forum where criticism can be directly refuted, to ensure their arguments are to the point of science and logic, and to refrain from attacks based on perceived slights with conformity or insufficient inclusiveness in a pet scientific field. There will also no doubt be righteous scorn, indignation, and ridicule heaped on by political conservatives and perhaps religionists (on the evolution aspects) whom this book may offend. There will be somehow found a way to deal with these as well. There is no need, however, for anti-religion undertones to be part of any environmental agenda. I was educated from Kindergarden through Grade 6 in a Thunder Bay, Ontario Catholic school (St. Margaret's), including under the tutelage of nuns, and though I would hardly any longer consider myself a Catholic, will admit to the draw that some scripture occasionally still holds. In light of that and in the spirit of inclusiveness, the beginning of some chapters hold a verse that seems to fit the topic, from ones that were identified by Christian ecologists (a group that should be more recognized by Christian conservatives and less religious ones also as truly shining a light in the right direction).

Luke 12:15,23,34. And He said to them, "Beware and be on your guard against every form of greed; for not even when one has an abundance does life consist of his possessions. For life is more than food, and the body more than clothing. For where your treasure is, there will your heart be also.

CHAPTER 1

Conservative Politics and the Environment (Say It Ain't So)

It is clear now to most people that human activities have disrupted the ecological balance of the planet through global climate change, as well as resulted in heavy pollution in the air, water, and the degradation of soil in many parts of the country and world. The climate change issue actually constitutes a threat to our continued survival as a species, at least under the conditions as we have so far experienced them. Small changes in climate-change policy and management, as have so far been implemented in parts of the world, have brought forth very little if anything to show for them.

European nations and others have at least made some efforts to abide by the quite weak restrictions in the global climate agreements established so far, but they have actually achieved very little. The United States, a major and influential player in global climate change and in the efforts to reach international agreements, has through the US Senate consistently vetoed progressive environmental requirements, based on the perception that they would have potentially negative effects to the US economy. Conservatives (Republicans mainly) in Congress have stymied any meaningful reduction of pollutants important in climate change, and as well have been instrumental in impeding progress in other domestic environmental areas. A change in the United States' recalcitrant position in the global climate talks or in other domestic areas would require major changes in national environmental policy. This would require a significant shift in social policy and politics.

A huge impediment in bringing this shift about is a factor rarely discussed openly during consideration of environmental policy, but to continue to ignore it at this crucial time would be irresponsible. This is that the profit interests of commerce and industry are promoted most vigorously by political conservatives, who also happen to be fundamentally opposed to more regulations in general, especially those that can hamper industry profit interests. It is therefore political conservatives in concert with corporate industry who have always obstructed environmental advancements in this country. This alliance is currently impeding progress in this area and is likely to continue doing so in the future, and with the US's remaining influence in global environmental issues, it will continue to be the obstructive force against any meaningful climate-change legislation.

Of course, there are many other great environmental threats, including freshwater purity and availability, waste disposal, air pollution, overgrazing, land clearing, and the continuing extinction of species. A huge issue is population growth, with its associated environmental effects. It's obviously an issue fraught with religious and conservative sensitivities. All of these environmental aspects can be considered relevant to the discourse of this book. There are other issues with respect to social policy, mainly economic, briefly addressed below and more so at the end, but we will focus mainly on the environmental policies for which these ideas were originally developed.

Considering environmental deterioration and climate change, it should be clear to any thinking realist that sufficient improvements will totally depend on the establishment of significantly more intensive or protective environmental regulations than are present now. Industries that are doing most of the polluting obviously won't cut it down voluntarily, since they've had plenty of opportunity for doing so but have instead fought against tighter regulations and better pollution controls from day one. And industry wouldn't have been able to fight as effectively as it has if not for its alliances with conservatives in Congress. Of course, this is nothing new, and environmentalists have their liberal supporters in government. One or the other of the two sides has held more sway at some point or on some issue in the past, here in the United States and elsewhere. The difference now is that in many environmental areas and especially with respect to climate change, we are at a critical juncture. The regulatory situation will have to change, and significantly, or there could be irreversible, long-lasting and significant effects on our environment and it will affect every one of us.

Regional environmental improvements in the United States and elsewhere, such as real improvements in water and air quality have actually occurred, but only through the early breakthrough national laws and regulations such as the Clean Air Act and Clean Water Act, passed in the 1970s (under Richard Nixon, a Republican president). These were passed only after a broad recognition that our environment was seriously deteriorating and environmental degradation had resulted in widespread public disgust, such as after the Cuyahoga River in Ohio caught on fire from the industrial pollutants in it. Events like that tend to concentrate the public mind. One can only wonder what event or series of events might bring on the next stage of grand environmental awareness in the public (but we are getting ahead of ourselves).

There are two main questions that arise from the above discussion, and they were investigated under the scientific method and in the most logical sense the author could muster. The first is how important really is this political factor of conservative distaste for more regulation in regards to the actual implementation of environmental reform. The second, linked and two-part question is how and why have our political philosophies developed to include in large proportion[1] (40 percent of Americans describe their political views as conservative, 35 percent as moderate, and 21 percent as liberal) one philosophy that acts in apparent detriment to the protection of our environment, and what does this imply for the establishment of more effective environmental policy? The scientific method includes making conjectures (hypotheses), deriving logical predictions from them, testing the predictions, and finally analyzing the results and drawing conclusions. The answer to the first question, as will be illustrated directly, is that this political factor is a huge issue in establishing effective environmental reform, in both a national perspective and in terms of global climate change. The conclusion reached regarding question two is that our two major opposing political philosophies (liberalism and conservatism) have evolved directly from the two major primal behavioral response mechanisms (cooperation and competition) in an evolutionarily logical progression. The implications of this, in answer to the second part of the question, are that these political philosophies exist as part of innate behavioral (neural) complexes, and in individuals characterized as being at the farther right, conservative end of the political spectrum (as with those on the far left), views are typically very firmly held. (We will not be concerned here with the views of the far left since these typically are strongly protective toward the environment and are therefore not an issue in this regard.) So, if this is indeed the case, it can be expected that firm resistance to heightened environmental regulation by groups representing conservative interests will, unfortunately, continue unabated into the foreseeable future.

Before going into the evolutionary and social science basis for the theory, we first need to look at the founding assumption, which is that political conservatives have typically blocked, and will continue to attempt to block, any significant new environmental regulation. This phenomenon applies in many countries, especially Western ones, but we will consider here mainly the United States, at least for the sake of focus. Since the United States also is the leading voice globally as a superpower and thus in global climate-change policy, this is not a debilitating restriction. Political decisions on environmental issues have been marked by tension between the political left (liberals) and right (conservatives), with the latter typically displaying considerably less concern for the environment than the former. It can be easily shown that political conservatives have consistently blocked or tried to block environmental reforms. This is not to say that all conservatives have always voted against all environmental reforms, but that the vast majority of their actions have been along these lines. The preponderance of historical evidence illustrates this readily, going back to the promulgation of the first US air and water pollution legislation, wetlands protection, industrial chemicals regulation, etc. The US Clean Air and Clean Water Acts, the Fish and Wildlife Coordination Act, the National Environmental Policy Act, the Resource Conservation and Recovery Act, and others (as well as their promulgating regulations) all have registered vociferous objections from industry and their conservative legislative supporters during their public review process, and this opposition can be viewed in the records. The positions taken in more modern times by conservatives in Congress almost unilaterally, and in the White House for the most part (with a few exceptions), have been in opposition to environmental reform. This is easily seen in voting records, in bills proposed and passed, and in other documentation, as discussed further below.

As was noted, it is the typical and preponderant views and actions that are at play here, and the recent trend has been a movement even further to the right in the Republican Party (among the more conservative members and the recent Tea Party movement). To be sure, many conservatives in the Democratic Party, and some centrist and even the self-proclaimed liberal members, have supported at times the above economic interests even when they are at odds with best environmental policy. For Democrats, this is most often due to regional economic factors that include labor and other regional issues, and undoubtedly, in general, due to the corrupting influence of current US campaign finance practices. Large corporations, including energy companies and utilities, industry, and the megabanks have essentially purchased many (most?) members of Congress in the House and Senate through campaign contributions and favors. Nevertheless, usually when serious, fundamental environmental issues arise, such as climate-change legislation, voting has in the past proceeded and can most likely be counted on in the future to proceed as described above, with most Republicans and almost all, if not all, conservatives typically voting against them.

Although congressional voting records are extensive, a reliable source has not been found that has evaluated them specifically by ideological groupings. Conducting such a review is beyond the scope and need of this book; nevertheless, examples from specific cases, as well as from other readily available documentation, are telling. A specific case occurring at the time of this writing (starting around 2007) in regards to blocking the regulation of hazardous chemicals is a good example. Under the Toxic Substances Control Act, manufacturers must report to the federal government any new chemicals they intend to market, but the law has exempted revealing information that could potentially harm the companies' bottom line. The American Chemistry Council, supported mainly by conservative, pro-corporate legislators, successfully argued at that time that the federal government should not only keep the names of their chemicals secret but also hide from public view the identities of the manufacturers. Government scientists and environmental groups have since claimed that manufacturers have exploited weaknesses in the law to exempt an ever-increasing number of chemicals, so new legislation to expand disclosure was proposed. The legislation was actively opposed by the American Chemistry Council, which is supported again mainly by conservative, pro-business legislators, led by the conservative Republican senator James Inhofe, who was the ranking member of the Environment and Public Works Committee. Inhofe testified that the law was basically fine as it was. Championing the majority, the liberal Democratic senator Barbara Boxer stated that this was an opportunity to strengthen the nation's laws on toxic substances to ensure that people are protected. The vote went along party lines.

Similar votes, also almost exclusively along party lines, have characterized all recent climate-change bills introduced in the US Congress. The Kerry-Boxer Bill (S. 1733: Clean Energy Jobs and American Power Act) passed the Senate Environment and Public Works Committee in 2009 with no Republican participation (it was later dropped, with Senator Kerry moving on to work on a different bill that was hoped would pass all of Congress). The Waxman-Markey bill (HR 2454: American Clean Energy and Security Act) has been the most ambitious cap-and-trade bill so far and also the most successful, having passed in the House in June 2009. The voting went thus: Democrats were 210 for the bill and 43 against; Republicans were 8 for and 169 against. Of the 43 no votes by Democrats, approximately 15 each were in either Southern, conservative states like Alabama, Georgia, and Texas, or in Mid-American coal-energy states like Indiana, Illinois, and Pennsylvania. It is hard for politicians from coal states, or from states whose utilities use a lot of coal, to vote for bills with carbon caps or that will otherwise significantly increase energy costs initially for their constituents. There were obviously other (and self-defeating) reasons for some Democrats to vote no, including, apparently, for staunch environmentalists like Congressman Kucinich of Ohio and Congressman DeFazio of Oregon, that the bill did not go nearly far enough in rolling back climate change and was therefore not worth voting for. On the other hand, all of the eight Republicans who voted yes are from mainly Democratic (liberal) states like California, New York, and New Jersey. The vast majorities on both sides, however, voted along party lines, with the more liberal party voting for the legislation and the more conservative one voting against.

Other available documentation includes the positions of self-proclaimed conservative and liberal think tanks and institutions on climate-change policy. The Brookings Institution, a liberal organization, has articles on its website (at the time of this writing) that are proactive toward climate-change legislation, including two entitled, "Time for a Price Collar on Carbon," and "On the Merits of a Carbon Tax." The Heritage Foundation, a conservative think tank, has (had) the following articles on its website: "Proposed Global Warming Bills and Regulations Will Do More Harm

Than Good," and "Climate Policy: Free Trade Promotes a Cleaner Environment." The titles speak for themselves. Another aspect of political ideological leanings regarding the environment can be seen in the political platforms of the two major US political parties. At the time of this initial writing, prior to the 2008 national election, the priority that the more liberal, Democratic Party, gave to the environment can be compared to that given by the more conservative, Republican Party. The 2008 platforms (2012 updates below) of Democrats and Republicans clearly prioritized environmental issues quite differently and fall in line with the positions suggested above. The Democratic Party's platform had the environment listed as a key issue, and the platform went into some detail about global climate change and offered suggestions for addressing it, including passing "cap and trade" legislation to cut US emissions of greenhouse gases.

The Republican Party's 2008 platform contained a plethora of conflicting positions and in many ways mimicked the party's political objections to real climate-change legislation. Its position was for using market-driven, technology-based solutions to "eliminate climate change where it occurs." (Where it occurs? Hint, does "global" ring a bell?) Of course, it also stated that any treaty <u>obligations</u> must be "global" in nature, which, of course, provides a convenient out as long as some developing countries are not yet participating. (As long as the "developing" countries of Russia, China, and India do not fully participate in global gas-reduction agreements, it gives conservatives in this country an out. There is some basis for this, of course, since there are large and growing pollutant inputs from these nations, and they should not be let totally off the hook. But they have in fact not been part of the problem in much of the global buildup over the last century compared to the United States, the United Kingdom, and Europe, and provision is being made in the global discussions that will require phasing in the developing countries' commitment. This, as we'll see, however, is not satisfactory for conservatives.)

At the same time, the Republican platform goes on, the approach must not be centrally planned, since this would perilously empower Washington, and the advantages of private ownership in protecting the environment must be appreciated over centralized command-and-control measures. It's not clear how the US government should participate with no centralized approach. Perhaps we should just eliminate the middleman and let private industry represent us in those talks? The platform does not require any sacrifice economically for the American people or any change to their lifestyles. The document was nice-sounding but obfuscating and self-limiting, full of pie-in-the-sky, market-oriented, do-nothing approaches that repudiate even the smallest loss in profits or change in lifestyle. It did not actually address any of the real environmental problems.

Updating this subject to the 2012 political platforms, the issue of climate change essentially disappears from the Republican platform. In a response to a debate question from the American Association for the Advancement of Science (AAAS), the party's presidential candidate, Mitt Romney, wrote that "there remains a lack of scientific consensus on the issue..." and restated the concern about other emitters' participation before any real commitment can occur. But the platform does urge Congress to "take quick action" to prevent the EPA from regulating greenhouse gas emissions! There must also, of course, be many additional studies conducted before any precipitous actions are taken.

The Democratic platform retreated from cap-and-trade legislation to cut US emissions of greenhouse gases and instead proposed to negotiate a "binding and enforceable" international agreement to curb global warming. It continued to call climate change "one of the biggest threats of this generation" and mocks the opposition's move so far to the right "as to doubt the science of climate change." President Obama, in his nomination acceptance speech at the Democratic National Convention, said that "climate change is not a hoax," alluding to some conservatives' stated opinions on the issue. The platform contains no new policy prescriptions but pledges to work toward agreement to "set emission limits in unison with other emerging powers" (giving apparent ground to the canard of the participation of emerging powers as a requirement, in a sense retreating a little more. (We can perhaps hope that the appointment of Senator Kerry as US Secretary of State will bring some improvement here).

We can list many more similar legislative and other examples of conservatives blocking environmental regulatory reform, but in truth, this is understood fundamentally by anyone with minimal political sophistication, and should be acknowledged readily if given honest consideration. I would dare any thinking person to say it ain't so! In fact, most conservatives themselves would acknowledge it in some degree (of course, short of admitting that stopping regulations would actually result in any real environmental harm). The reasons most often given by conservatives for objecting to environmental regulation are that the proposed regulations go too far or are advocated by groups too radical to be taken seriously (relating to concerns about threats to constitutional freedoms), and that they cost too much (relating to economic freedoms). Boiled down, the most serious objections heard in political discussions to regulatory restrictions are the economic ones of cost and the threat to free-market competition. This philosophy obviously lends itself to common bonds with industrial, commercial, and financial corporations and interests, and the above voting records and other legislative actions clearly reflect it.

A brief foray into economic policy in the United States relating to conservative politics was promised, and though this might at first be thought somewhat beyond an environmental scope, the connections regarding allocation of scarce economic resources and environmental controls should be obvious. Without going too far into economic theory and practice, the point can be easily made that conservatives, through their staunch insistence on deregulation have been in many ways a deleterious force here also. Many economists have concluded that the deregulation of large financial institutions, has resulted in almost ruining the country's—and the world's—financial stability in the 2008 Great Recession. Free-market economic theory, as held strongly mainly by conservatives, is the impetus behind the long drive and final success in repealing a banking law passed following the Great Depression, the Glass-Steagall Act of 1933. The act required the major change that investment business could not be conducted by firms that also offered the public traditional retail savings and loans services. The repeal of this law only about ten years ago set up the conditions for the financial collapse of 2008 and the economic collapse and unemployment that still exist in the United States and much of the world. More will be said about this near the end of the book, since the author has followed the economics and finances of this issue with much personal interest. It also seems obvious that the economy will have a very large impact on how and to what degree our continuing limited resources will be spent in improving the environment.

Ezekiel 34:2-4. Woe to the shepherds of Israel who only take care of themselves! Should not the shepherds take care of the flock? You eat the curds, clothe yourselves with the wool and slaughter the choice animals, but you did not take care of the flock! You have not strengthened the weak or healed the sick or bound up the injured. You have not brought back the strays or searched for the lost. You have ruled them harshly and brutally.

CHAPTER 2

The Art and Science of Cooperation

As a kind of introduction to this chapter it may be helpful to first summarize the overall scientific theory of the book, which this chapter begins and is an important part of. The investigation into the questions raised initially required crossing over into various scientific fields, including evolution science, paleoanthropology, and psychology. A review of the scientific literature in those disciplines revealed that there are likely direct evolutionary linkages between primal behavioral mechanisms and modern political philosophies. A note (mainly for potential scientific critics claiming non-inclusiveness): there has been no attempt to encompass the extensive body of work that has been done in the branches of science relating to cooperation theory, nor in the evolution and social sciences of the following chapters. As noted in the Introduction and restated here: to even have attempted that would have been ludicrous. A few studies have been selected, from many others that could have been chosen, that support the scientific contentions in the book and help elucidate the relevant science and theory in the disciplines involved. There are responsibilities that should be shouldered by any potential critics complaining that some important aspect was omitted, or that the theory is discredited by a countervailing finding or by their interpretation of the science. These include the need to ensure that the criticism is to the substance of the science, and also to include a reasonable alternate approach to the one described here, and which would be supported by the criticism given.

Recent work in evolutionary neurobehavioral biology has greatly increased our understanding of how modern human neurobehavioral networks have evolved (Chapter 3). In addition, psychologists (Chapter 4) have uncovered psychological and physiological links and indicators for political philosophies; studies with twins have examined the strength of partisan political leanings; and genetic models have been applied to examine the sources and intensity of identification with political parties.

The above large bodies of work in those fields are underlain by some very insightful studies in paleoanthropology and of ancestral cooperation behaviors. The indications from all of these studies are that political philosophies can be linked and traced back to corresponding specific organization within neural networks. Thus, political philosophies closely associated with either more liberal or conservative ideologies are typically quite strongly held, to the extent in some cases regardless of obvious countering data and information. Political conservatives seem to exhibit this behavior strongly, and demonstrate consistent opposition to stronger environmental or climate-change policy and regulation, even in the face of clear evidence of its great necessity.

But why have humans evolved to a point where our brains and capabilities have become powerful enough to create earth-changing technologies, and yet are apparently unable to prevent the harmful effects of these technologies to seriously impact our planet? It seemed apparent to the author that more political consensus for environmental regulatory reform would require a generally higher level of a cooperative type of behavior than now exists in our politics and society.

Cooperative behavior in this sense is thought of as working together toward a goal, such as protecting the environment, as opposed to competing with others for scarce resources, such as food sources, farmland, water, or, of course, money and power. Since cooperation is one of the basic behavioral tendencies in humans and other animals, and competition the other, the question arose as to whether there could be a connection between these tendencies and our current political philosophies; that is, are the characteristics of our current political philosophies traceable to our ancestral behavioral mechanisms, and if so, what does that mean?

As might be expected, there is much scientific literature on both of the primal behavioral mechanisms, and on their existence in many biological species besides humans. Cooperation has been tested for and widely accepted to exist in many biological systems and in human evolution. Competition (the term used throughout here but alternately can be related to aggression, selfishness, and conflict) is obviously widely recognized and accepted as a basic mechanism for evolution and natural selection, so comparatively much less attention will be given to it here.

Darwin had problems with his finding of altruism (a principle form of cooperative behavior in which individuals act to help others at some cost to themselves) since it appeared to refute the basis of his theory, survival of the fittest and competition at every level. Though generally avoided today for obvious reasons, the linkages between evolution science and politics go back quite far. In a recent book on altruism,[2] the author describes how the differences between T.H. Huxley—"Darwin's bulldog"—and Russian biologist Peter Kropotkin over whether altruism is strictly kin-based or more widely found in nature, were highly influenced by their own political views. Victorian England in Huxley's time was even then a relatively heavily populated place where competition was central to all aspects of life, including reliance on a strong military, a capitalistically oriented economy, and a competitive education system. Huxley saw Darwin's work as exhibiting nature as a constant struggle for survival, red in tooth and claw.

Russia, meanwhile, in that time, though hardly peaceful, was mainly a land of lightly populated vast spaces where social-istic and anarchistic tendencies were widespread, and Kropot-kin observed what looked to him like nature in a high state of cooperation everywhere. The species he observed in that large, cold landscape seemed to be cooperating actively and altruisti-cally through necessity, and not only based on kin or relatedness between individuals.

From those early discussions and work, evolutionary studies in cooperation and its major sub-category, altruism became increas-ingly specialized. (We will continue to use the terms somewhat interchangeably in keeping with how various studies described below use them, but the reader should understand that one is nevertheless a subgroup of the other.) "Group selection" was pos-tulated as the main method by which altruism evolved, that is by favorable selection of traits that mainly benefited the group, and not necessarily only for related individuals. The renowned evo-lutionist William David Hamilton (who died in 2000 and whose ideas are still being avidly debated in the field) organized con-cepts from previous studies in population genetics by biologists such as the American Sewall Wright and the Englishmen Ronald

Fisher and J.B.S. Haldane. (These last three in fact founded the discipline of population genetics, which integrates natural selection with Mendelian genetics and was the critical first step in developing the modern unified synthesis theory of evolution.)

Hamilton assigned a mathematical basis for altruism by developing a simple relationship using a "relatedness" factor between individuals (from Wright) and the estimated costs and benefits of particular types of altruism to predict whether it would actually occur. The not unexpected results were that the greater the relatedness, the greater the chance of altruistic behavior. This seemed to settle for a time the question of kin selection versus the existence of other mechanisms for altruism, but Robert Trivers[3] made a strong case for non-kin, "reciprocal" altruism. The "relatedness" issue was later refined by Richard Dawkins,[4] who proposed (from one of Hamilton's previous suggestions) that it is the evolutionary success of the gene, not necessarily that of the individual organism, that drives not only selective competition but cooperative and altruistic behaviors also.

Although the specific evolutionary selection mechanisms for cooperation are still being debated among scientists (these being mainly population structure, group selection, kin selection, direct and indirect reciprocity, and costly signaling), cooperative behavior in general has been found in many different species of organisms, from the higher animals and insect societies that are most familiar, to primitive biological systems, like slime molds and bacterial viruses,[5] to even sub-cellular systems.[6] We don't need to get into the weeds on the details of these studies, but let it just be said that the scientists who conducted them are recognized in their fields and feel quite confident about their results, as amazing as they might seem to us. (Of course, readers should feel free to delve into them to their satisfaction from the references given.)

Many important findings on human cooperation theory resulted from a prototype computer-based tournament devised by the American political scientist Robert Axelrod, working with W.D. Hamilton, that challenged experts in relevant fields to submit their best strategies to win a game of Prisoner's Dilemma.[7] The game is based on realistic conditions: two prisoners charged in a crime are offered a reward, reduced punishment, for defecting and informing on the other. The two choices each prisoner has then are to defect from his partner and "squeal," or to cooperate with him by remaining silent. The game was carried out by assigning numerical values to each choice and then computing the results of many possible iterative interactions, carried out to a total of 120,000 moves. The challenge was issued to professional game theorists who knew the game and could develop a computer program to win it. Fourteen entries were submitted from five disciplines: psychology, economics, political science, mathematics, and sociology.

The surprising finding was that if the game was played long enough, the simplest cooperative strategy always seemed to come out the winner, even though competitive strategies often were exhibited at the beginning. This cooperative strategy was called tit for tat, which essentially was that a response by one participant was always met with a reciprocal (same) response. A defection was always met with a defection and cooperation was also always reciprocated.

Despite the contention of other more complicated strategies, including many variations of competitive ones, under the conditions of the game, tit for tat always scored higher than all of the others. Axelrod further developed these initial findings with other tests he conducted using more complex conditions, for example, to represent the changing ecological conditions in the natural environment. In all cases, given some basic conditions such as the game being played long enough, the cooperative tit-for-tat strategy always came out the winner.

In his interesting book, *A Brief History of the Mind: From Apes to Intellect and Beyond,*[8] W.H. Calvin notes that during the hard climactic times for early humans, cooperative behaviors were probably enhanced by the need to increase hunting efficiency, and for food preparation of otherwise inedible plants. The preponderance of grasslands during much of these early periods tended to concentrate and greatly increase the herds of grazers that were the most important prey of early hunters, but even these conditions required cooperation among relatively weak and slow humans. Cooperation among these early humans was probably, by the time of the Upper Paleolithic at least, also enhanced by the fact that the relatively large sizes of animals killed[9] allowed for sharing among a group, including groups (bands) containing several families.

This process also likely included the beginning of the influence of reciprocity in human cooperative behavior. It was undoubtedly important to know who was actually pulling his or her share, in either the hunting or other work that was required, and thereby increasing the probability of success for the group. Non-altruists were ostensibly "removed" by altruists within bands, and this has been termed "selective assortment."[10] Game theorists since Axelrod have shown that punishment of free riders (which can be costly to the punisher as well as the punished) can result in increasingly reduced costs to punishers when it is coordinated with increasing numbers of others, and when it is relatively rare.[11] When human groups began the practice of herding domesticated animals, Calvin writes, it probably reinforced sensitivity to the concept of ownership, and increased competitive drives associated with domestication.

In spite of the above work and others indicating the probability that altruism toward other group members would improve the overall fitness of the group, some researchers have not fully accepted the biological evolution of altruism in humans. The main reason given is that competition between individuals is likely to increase if a group becomes isolated, and so altruistic behavior would then decrease an individual's level of fitness compared with other members. Another assumption is that hunter-gatherer groups around this time period would not have been sufficiently genetically related to favor altruism, so that when altruists died when defending the group their genes would die with them.

A large study[12] by the well-known American behavioral scientist Samuel Bowles of the Santa Fe Institute had many interesting findings in early human development, and put the above skepticism into somewhat of a retreat. It was done by assembling genetic, climactic, archaeological, ethnographic, and experimental data and information to examine cost-benefit relationships and potentials for the evolution of human cooperation in ancient populations. Genetic analyses were conducted of contemporary hunter-gatherers, including Australian aboriginals, native Siberian Inuits, and indigenous tribal groups in Africa (it is assumed by researchers that these modern-day groups still live much like our distant ancestors did).

The genetic variation in these groups was analyzed and used to estimate the kind of variation that would have existed in ancestral populations of hunter-gatherers from the Pleistocene and early Holocene (circa 150,000 to ten thousand years ago). What Bowles found was that early humans were likely to be substantially more interrelated within groups than previously thought, and also that larger genetic differences than expected existed between discrete groups of ancient peoples. He suggested the latter would have favored altruistic behavior through the selective extinction of non-altruistic groups.

From a genetic standpoint and in his model, these groups are called "demes," isolated subpopulations of bands of humans living in those times. The median band size was estimated to be nineteen individuals (by census from archeological surveys), and five bands were estimated to make up most demes. Archaeological sites from the late Pleistocene suggest that lethal conflicts occurred often and that violence intensified during periods of climatic adversity and resource stress, mainly food-source scarcity and therefore the need to compete with other groups for these resources. He claims his work showed that culturally transmitted practices such as food sharing and monogamy could have leveled out the "cost" of altruistic behavior.

Food sharing can obviously be considered costly in one sense for individuals who may be confident in their abilities to obtain it, but it can just as obviously be quite worth it when an individual or family falls into a spell of bad luck in any number of ways. In his model, though deme members bearing genes for altruistic behavior might have been burdened by limiting their reproductive opportunities (monogamy was assumed to be associated with altruism), they benefited from sharing food and information, thereby increasing the average fitness of the group as well as their interrelatedness. Monogamy, Bowles suggested, would also level the playing field within the group by limiting the ability of the stronger or more aggressive males to monopolize copulation.

Bowles claimed his work indicated that it is mainly with respect to genetic differentiation that even infrequent inter-deme conflict would have been sufficient to spread costly forms of altruism. More simply put, because the genetic differences between groups were substantial, even if conflicts between them were infrequent, those who were more successful because they fought together better would win out, evolutionarily, against those who were less cooperative within the group. So, the advantage of being in a group having more cooperative genes, because they survived better against other groups, far outweighed the "cost" of the cooperative behavior on an individual basis within the group. (This certainly is a strategy widely employed today by sports team coaches, who stress the importance of working for the benefit of the team, and downplaying individual glory. It is also a characteristic widely approved of by sports fans around the world.) Bowles suggests that the initial spread of altruism among humans could have occurred by just a few of the vast number of late Pleistocene demes (because of their comparative evolutionary advantages). He also suggests that reproductive leveling (food sharing and monogamy), could have provided an evolutionary pathway or a genetic predisposition for culturally transmitted practices carrying altruistic behaviors to have evolved. In other words, the process of successful altruists breeding more successful altruists begins to lay down a pathway for the behavior to become instilled, in a large part, culturally. (In the conclusion we will discuss whether and to what degree cooperative behaviors in general may have begun to overtake our primal competitive strategies in some circumstances or cultures.)

So, based on all the above as a mere sampling of the available relevant information, cooperation appears to be an intrinsic life strategy that is operating at a very basic level and is also widely exhibited. And, as evidenced by the vast proliferation of life on this planet, cooperation strategies have obviously had a great measure of evolutionary success. It's clear that competition has also been an important and widely distributed strategy for survival and evolution, and is, of course, most evident in survival of the fittest, a driving force for natural selection, the process underlying Darwin's great discovery of biological evolution.

Competition is the term used here for the opposite side of cooperation, and can be considered the catchall for this drive that has also been described as aggression, conflict, or selfishness. Competitiveness would have been an important strategy very early on in human history with respect to controlling the best hunting/gathering areas, gaining resources for tool-making, winning of mates, and other needs. Although competition in the classical sense we are discussing it here is probably a commonly understood phenomenon, it might help to focus on that meaning more precisely as "an active demand by two or more organisms or kinds of organisms for some <u>environmental</u> resource in short supply." As with cooperation, however, it must be remembered that the behavioral mechanism of competition can be complex and can include different types, including destructive (zero sum) and non-destructive, or even cooperative types (such as cooperation among individuals or groups against other groups, as in Bowles above).

To look at it from a more philosophical perspective[13], it has been said that competitive drive must be distinguished from what are, in some cases, evolutionary benefits that can be attributed to competition per se', but not in the form that many may think of as a competitive drive. Some species have benefited in some instances from nonaggressive actions in an overall competitive evolution, such as finding a better food source, evolving camouflage, or even moving away from or cooperating with other species (as in competition for regional resources with a third species). The benefits of these actions or traits can be seen as arising from competitive forces, but the actual competitive or aggressive drive can be minimal or even nonexistent in the classical sense.

In fact, few animals exhibit extensive interspecies, or even intra-species aggression. Even well-known types of aggression, such as that between rival males over access to females, is limited in that rarely does either combatant get seriously injured or die, probably because, as in predation, overly risky behavior would have negative survival benefits. Nevertheless, owing to its widely acknowledged role as a basic behavioral foundation for survival, we can rightly focus here primarily on the classic, primal, destructive type best known as defining competitive behavior. It should also be acknowledged that both strategies—competition and cooperation—have played if not equal then definitely the two major roles in shaping our biological and cultural evolution. And as we will see in coming chapters, these primal behavioral "strategies" continue to play a strong role in how we now, in our cultural sophistication, view environmental issues, including of course climate change.

Romans 1:19-20. For what can be known about God is plain to them, because God has shown it to them. Ever since the creation of the world His eternal power and divine nature, invisible though they are, have been understood and seen through the things He has made. So they are without excuse

CHAPTER 3

Neurobehavioral Evolution

Let's for a moment review where we are and revisit the main biological aspects of the theory presented in this book. A logical assumption from the scientific work that will be further described below is that the two primal, somewhat opposing behavioral response mechanisms, cooperation and competition, were hard-wired into our neurobehavioral mechanisms and networks. Then, as our brains, practices, and cultures evolved into more complex forms, these mechanisms adapted to the changing environmental and cultural conditions. Those experiences and practices led to evolutionary adaptations in our brains, coupled with rewiring and proliferation of the existing neurobehavioral mechanisms and networks, and thus were "wired" in as well. As these adaptations continued to evolve, they most likely built onto or reorganized with the existing structures, since this would be most efficient from an evolutionary standpoint. This would mean that the neural reorganization of the new adaptations would be built onto the preexisting, respective, ancestral neuronal structures responsible for cooperative and competitive behaviors. The adaptations would thus maintain, probably to a high degree, the somewhat opposing nature and characteristics of the primal behavioral cognitive complexes that existed as they evolved. (There is an evolutionary concept suggested by some scientists called "exaptation," where basically a totally new function will be taken up by a structure or trait not previously owning it, which could provide an alternate possibility. This is discussed briefly later but does not materially affect the theory described here).

Evolutionary biologists coined the term "norms of reaction," which in the standard definition are patterned responses to a range of environmental input factors or variations. For example, some male insects are more likely to guard their mates when there are fewer females in the population, hence fewer mating opportunities for other males. Natural selection didn't initially result in a fixed behavior (guarding their mates only when there were fewer of them around); it allowed for the norm of reaction, the nature of the response. It used the neural framework that was already there, the drive to mate and then to guard the mate, and then later assimilated onto that drive an adaptation to improve fitness. The males more avidly guard their mate when there are fewer females, thereby ensuring better mating success while also conserving valuable energy. There is no need to waste energy flying around defending a female when there are a lot of them available, and hence less competition for any one of them. (Not a bad situation for males of any species lucky enough to find themselves in.)

An example of a behavioral adaptation closer to our subject (humans) can be conceived from our archeological history. An early form of cooperative hunting was banding together to drive a herd of grazers toward a group of waiting hunters, or over a cliff (where there would be basically carcasses waiting to be butchered). The higher level of cooperation needed to plan and coordinate, for example, the erection of barricades to funnel the herd more efficiently and improve the chances of success would have obviously built upon the preexisting behavior. It would not have just sprung up out of the blue. Early humans probably more quickly evolved higher intelligence largely due to this kind of interactive planning and communication[14]. There can be little doubt that almost any adaptation one can think of that increases the complexity of preexisting behaviors would do likewise, maintaining the fundamental characteristics of the prewired neural pathways associated with the existing forms of those behaviors or functions.

It's evident that these kinds of behavioral adaptations would have continued to increase in complexity as needed, eventually forming, in the case of cooperative and competitive behavioral mechanisms (among other behavioral outcomes), the forerunners of our modern political philosophies. Looking back over human history, there is little reason to believe our cultural behavioral adaptations would not have proceeded as described above. Paleoanthropologic data on prehistoric human cultures (such as was reviewed by Calvin and Bowes) along with historic information on human societies point to the likelihood that human cultures increased in complexity incrementally (though obviously varying among different cultures and with varying rates through time in general[15]). Thus there would have been no reason for our adaptive behavioral mechanisms not to have followed suit; that is, progressively evolving by adding layering or associative complexing of adaptive functions onto preexisting neurobehavioral foundations.

The manner in which these types of elements evolved in relation to function has been the subject of much recent study. Neuroscientists Bittman and Friedman conducted an extensive review[16] of currently available data in neuroscience, evolutionary biology, and evolutionary psychology. They developed a genetic-based model that predicts that humans and other animals have evolved many non-universal (species-typical) behaviors, or "natures." Their model suggests that complex adaptations have many imperfections, different functions in different environments, and much genetic variation. The implication of this is the existence of multiple genetic human natures, which the authors say could have provided perhaps for the evolution of "natures" that reflect not only imperfections but also <u>maladaptations</u>.

Bruce Lahn and his associates investigated[17] the genetic factors of the dramatic increase in brain size and complexity during human evolution and corroborated to a large degree Bittman and Friedman's model. They examined the evolution of genes involved in a diverse range of neurobiological systems, counting the number of changes in their DNA sequences that altered the proteins they produced (and scaling the changes to the amount of evolutionary time they would have required). They found (contrary to a preexisting theory) that large numbers of genes are involved in human brain evolution, and that hundreds or thousands of mutations occurred in hundreds or thousands of genes, all within the relatively limited evolutionary time (twenty to twenty-five million years) leading to modern humans. Lahn and others have pointed to this study as evidence that evolution was speeded up when it came to the human brain, and that adaptations occurred continuously over that time. This rapid evolution most likely occurred via the most efficient process for such a large number of adaptations to take hold in relatively short time, which would be by building onto existing mechanisms and networks with a related function.

Genes do not specify behavior directly but rather code for molecular products they build that include those that govern the functioning of the brain, including the parts that control the expression of behavior. Researchers (Robinson et al.[18]) who have synthesized a number of recent findings in the genetic influences of behavior (and vice versa, it turns out, behavior influencing genes) believe that neurobiological mechanisms that operate to control social behavior at the genomic level are "conserved" (aspects of the trait or mechanism is maintained throughout its evolution). Although behaviors among species can obviously vary quite significantly, they state that the biological needs that drive these behaviors are deeply shared. Even though social behavior has clearly evolved multiple times, they believe it has probably done so within a framework of commonly existing neural mechanisms.

Two specific points made by the authors go to the heart of the argument in this book. First, neurobehavioral information is transduced (converted and communicated) within individual organisms by one or more primary sensory pathways, and these neural signals are processed and integrated in specific circuits of the brain via "conserved signal transduction and neuromodulatory systems" (my quotations). They also found that social signals themselves (i.e., from the environment, including the actions of other individuals) can trigger long-lasting epigenetic modifications of the genome, and that social experience can induce a range of changes in brain gene expression. Epigenetics is the study of the interface between the genome and the environment and refers to functionally relevant modifications to the genome that do not involve a change in the nucleotide (DNA) sequence, typically mediated through the protein milieu of the DNA, and which can nevertheless be inherited for several or more generations.

One of the studies reviewed that demonstrated epigenetic modification was on male zebra finches, where variations regarding recognition or not of a particular song of another male brings about a specific gene's expression in the auditory forebrain, which also is involved in social behavior linked to the songs. Familiar songs triggered expression by coding of a transcription factor (which specifies transfer of genetic code from DNA to messenger RNA, and subsequent direct manufacture of proteins such as neurotransmitters) linked to specific behavioral responses, which were mainly territorial in nature. The unfamiliar songs sometimes triggered similar responses, but the signal was stronger when the bird was in the presence of others of its species as opposed to when it was alone (the "audience effect"). This illustrates how genetics works interactively in evolution, not only in expressing the function of the existing neurosystem structures responsible for the behavior, as in building the neurotransducers involved, but also in changing the structure and function of these complexes through signals received from the environment. The presence of other males, which is an environmental factor, triggered the genetic expression through specific coding for neurotransmitter production that brought the behavioral response.

These are extremely interesting findings in elucidating the complex relationships between perception of environmental feedback, function, and existing structure via gene expression going on in our brains. They also clearly demonstrate a key idea expressed in this book: neurobehavioral mechanisms are conserved throughout evolution, with new concepts or more complex behaviors added or re-organized onto preexisting ones.

Regulation of these brain activities has been found to be through polypeptides, such as hormones, enzymes, and receptors. It was suggested by Ludwig and Leng[19] that neuropeptides, interacting with other neurotransmitter systems within specific neural circuits, may act either as neurotransmitters (at the site of neuron-to-neuron connections, the synapses), or as neurohormones activating receptors that may be distant from the site of their release. In a similar vein as the study discussed just above, they further state that these activities can in turn result in evolutionary capabilities, since some neuropeptide activities can result in a "temporary functional reorganization of neuronal networks" (again my quotations to highlight the point) containing specific peptide receptors, and thereby have the potential to result in more lasting changes. The finding provides more empirical support that our behavioral response mechanisms have evolved through adding complexity to preexisting neural function or structure.

Some interesting work relating neuropeptides to social behavior in vertebrates has focused on the powerful hormones oxytocin and vasopressin. Harking back for a moment to the last chapter and the early existence of cooperation in many organisms, Donaldson and Young[20] used game theory to look into the behavioral aspects of these neurochemicals. These reviewers noted that researchers using an established economic game found that participants with certain alleles (alternative forms of the same gene or genetic locus) for oxytocin receptors allocated more funds to another individual, despite the fact they would receive any unallocated funds at the end of the game in real money (which in these exercises is usually considered a good proof of concept). Complementary studies are also described in the paper whose results are consistent with a role for oxytocin in modulating feelings of trust, thereby influencing cooperative interactions. They also note that homologs (similar molecular forms) of oxytocin and vasopressin existed at least 700 million years ago and have been identified in such diverse organisms as hydra, worms, insects, and vertebrates such as us.

A final example is a recent perspective on cell signaling by Levy et al.[21] They reviewed work that described how protein kinases and phosphatases in budding yeast cells cooperate with other proteins and with each other in regulating both internal and external signals to decide response actions (for you biochemists out there, by phosphorylating or de-phosphorylating protein substrates). The reviewers noted that it would appear that evolutionary mechanisms must be at play for these relationships to have been set up, though they could not define the specifics. These last two perspectives provide unique examples of both cooperation at a sub-cellular level and of the continuous evolution of existing regulator systems. Living cells all use similar protein-interaction networks in cell decision making.

The results from the latter two studies, when added to the other findings above, show that conservation of behavioral mechanisms is a basic feature of our biological and cultural evolution:

First, there were many more mutations than previously thought that occurred during the rapid evolution of the human brain, these mutations relating to the number of neurostructural changes (adding complexity) over a limited geologic time (and hence most likely proceeded in the most efficient manner-incorporation onto existing mechanisms and networks);

Also, though there were many different "natures" that evolved, obviously for different life strategies, neurobehavioral information is transmitted within primary sensory pathways and is integrated in specific circuits of the brain via conserved neurobehavioral systems;

Neuropeptide transmitter activities can result in functional reorganization of neuronal networks;

Other neuropeptides, the homologs of oxytocin and vasopressin have been conserved over many_millions of years.

All of this work combined provides rigorous scientific support for the evolutionary aspect of the theory in this book: our existing political philosophies are a result of conserved primal behavioral neurosystems throughout our evolution, which evolved by adding complexity to the preexisting systems as our cultural environment changed and progressed. These more complex forms must have evolved eventually into the present widely and consistently distributed political philosophies. (At this point the reader will need to await the next chapter for the presentation of how the primal behavioral mechanisms are linked to their respective political philosophy traits.)

It has been assumed that some behavioral challenges, such as finding food, using language, learning to manipulate social competitors, etc., led to functions that led to structural developments in the brains of our australopithecine or early *Homo* ancestors. Some researchers (the late Gould and Vrba, others) have instead proposed a greater role for exaptation of structure to function (structure for a specific function or behavioral trait existed first on which a newly required function adapted). An example that has been cited may be the feather, which might have first evolved as a heat regulator, then may have been co-opted for display, then perhaps again co-opted, for flight. This chicken-or-egg argument of what came first, function or structure, is relevant to the thesis here only in terms of eventually dissecting the specific evolutionary progressions involved; its resolution is not required. Whatever the evolving behavioral function/structure steps were, the salient point is that the functions and structures evolved in a coupled and continuous fashion, building complexity as societal and cultural evolution progressed.

Of course, it is possible that many traits have evolved abruptly, as has been theorized by Gould and Lewontin in a process they named punctuated equilibrium. But that theory seeks to explain what the fossil record and other methods, including DNA and protein sequencing, appear to show as large, abrupt changes from preexisting forms. For the geologic time-paced evolution of ancestral behavioral mechanisms to complex philosophies (which is of course one of the main points in this book), there are no large leaps that need to be explained. It could have been, and in fact is far more likely, that this evolution was gradual and orderly, becoming ever more complex as our cultures became so. Incidentally, going back to the discussion in the introduction of why some people still won't believe in the science of evolution, the above methods of DNA and protein sequencing should by any rights put the final nail in that coffin. Of course, it would require actually doing the work of learning and understanding the science first before offhandedly denying it, apparently too large of an effort for the current crop of naysayers (or alternatively, it would require a little more than a total lack of interest in the actual science, which is probably the reality for the most part).

Job 12:7-10. But ask the animals, and they will teach you; or birds of the air and they will tell you; or speak to the earth and it will teach you; or let the fish of the sea inform you. Which of all these does not know that the hand of the Lord has done this. In His hand is the life of every creature and the breath of all mankind.

CHAPTER 4

The Psychology of Politics

The above discussion provides the evolutionary biological basis of the hypothesis, but what indicators are there to support the specific linkages suggested at the beginning (cooperation linked with liberalism, competition with conservatism)? I must admit, as a "hard" scientist, to an initial skepticism about the validity in trying to describe social political features in psychological (soft science) terms with a great deal of scientific rigor. I soon was impressed, however, by the extent and scientific vigor of the psychological studies that have been done, stretching back over fifty years. Social scientists have recently progressed quite far in describing liberal and conservative political philosophies in association with psychological and physiological variables. Here again it will be stated that there will be no attempt made to encompass the fairly extensive body of work done in this area. A few works have been selected that not only support the contentions in this book but also elucidate somewhat the prior and existing science and theory of the field.

As was seen in the previous chapters, review articles of the published literature by usually the top experts in the field are much handier to work with and explain in the context of this book, since in many or most cases the individual scientific articles themselves tend to be quite narrow in scope and focus on very tightly defined hypotheses (again relating to the scientific method). For this chapter of the book, especially, dealing with the psychological aspects of the theory, review studies are even more useful due to my admitted paucity of academic background in this area, as they help explain a body of work in ways most helpful. For the same reason, and even more so than in the preceding more traditional science-based chapters, I will stick even more closely to the conclusions drawn by the investigators, since venturing much further astray would no doubt quickly leave me looking down into nothing but air, Wile E. Coyote fashion.

A good transition point may be to first briefly mention an aspect of the relatively new field of evolutionary psychology (EP). Among the most cited writers in this field, the anthropologist John Tooby and his wife, the psychologist Leda Cosmides[22] have been credited with largely developing and first describing it. Since its roots are based in the principles of evolution, it is, of course, Charles Erasmus Darwin, whose writings touched on the evolutionary basis of human psychology, who is the real father of the field. In any case, a founding principle of EP is that behavior itself does not evolve, since evolution takes place between genes, which code for proteins, which build structures. Behaviors are functions associated with those structures. The mind, it is suggested in EP (and more widely), consists of structures in the brain that process information according to mechanisms that are functional, task-specific adaptations that have been selected for over the course of human evolution. As a reminder, these adaptations were established in response to the environmental and other conditions at the time the organism evolved, which may or may not be relevant or appropriate for the conditions at a later evolutionary time. These principles were introduced in the previous chapter, and this nugget of EP is included here mainly to give readers an idea of the vast amount of work that has been done in this field, which melds evolution science, neurobiology, and psychology.

As an opener to the field of psychology and political behaviors, we start with a study by Jost et al.[23] which is a meta-analytical review of a huge amount of previous work. The authors state that psychologists have been studying for decades the hypothesis that a variety of psychological motives and tendencies underlie ideological differences between the political left and right. They reviewed the voluminous literature that compares the cognitive styles and motivational needs of political conservatives with those of moderates, liberals, and left-wingers. They note that the studies of authoritarianism (the early categorization for conservatism) and other personality theories of political attitudes have often been controversial and have been dismissed as illegitimate and value-laden when they try to correlate psychological profiles with specific ideological beliefs. But that doesn't mean that researchers should avoid it. They claim that it is a legitimate empirical issue whether there are demonstrable links between a clearly defined set of psychological needs, motives, and properties and the adoption of politically conservative attitudes.

They use the term *motivated social cognition* to refer to a number of assumptions about the relationship between people's beliefs and their motivational underpinnings. Many different theoretical accounts of conservatism, they say, have stressed the motivational underpinnings of conservatism but have identified different needs as critical. Their review has used what they considered the best approach, linking the theories and findings of social and cognitive motives to the contents of specific political attitudes, and notes that it brings these diverse aspects together and integrates them for the first time.

The paper covers a lot of ground and includes numerous references. The following brief description includes information from the references given in the paper, and two of them are included in the references for this book (as sub-references under the cited article). One is for the major work referenced that was done by W.D. Wilson, an early and influential researcher, and the other for George F. Will, the right-wing columnist and panelist on many current political talk shows, from which several rather humorous (yes, from George Will!) citations were given.

Dictionary definitions of conservatism include "the disposition and tendency to preserve what is established; opposition to change" and "the disposition in politics to maintain the existing order." The authors believe that the two core dimensions of political conservatism are resistance to change and acceptance of inequality, and they note that though there are dramatic exceptions, these two are often generally psychologically related to one another for most of the (conservative) people most of the time. They base this partly on the historical fact that traditional social arrangements have generally been hierarchical as opposed to egalitarian. So, resisting change has often meant resisting increased efforts at egalitarianism, while preserving the status quo has typically meant entrusting the present and future to the same authorities who have controlled the past.

The paper integrates theories of personality (authoritarianism, dogmatism-intolerance of ambiguity), existential needs (for order, structure, and closure; regulatory focus; terror management), and ideological rationalization (social dominance, system justification) and links them to several psychological variables that predict defined aspects of political conservatism, such as anxiety of system instability, resistance to change, and justification of inequality. There is extensive information provided for most of the above aspects, which we will not go into very much here. It's fairly clear how variables such as anxiety of system instability and resistance to change relate to resistance to changes in a regulatory sense that can upset the existing economic system. Interestingly, the need for regulatory focus, as they discuss, is related mainly to law enforcement and keeping order, etc. (not to regulation of the "system" itself). Terror management, in their model, is related to death anxiety. It will probably be clearer to give what the authors summarized and concluded, and then try to provide some explanation on some of the perhaps more interesting aspects of the study.

The authors summarize that ideologies may be thought of as possessing a core and a periphery, and each may be fueled by separate motivational concerns. Also, they write that the most that can be expected of a general psychological analysis is for it to partially explain the core of political conservatism because the peripheral aspects are driven by historically changing, local contexts. They concluded that political conservatism is significantly related to motivational concerns having to do with the psychological management of uncertainty and fear. Specifically, the avoidance of uncertainty may be specifically tied to resistance to change. In addition, thoughts about fear and threat may be linked to the second core dimension of conservatism, endorsement of inequality. Although resistance to change and support for inequality are conceptually distinguishable, the authors believe that the two are psychologically interrelated, partly because motives pertaining to uncertainty and threat are interrelated. As was noted above, in past hierarchical societies, which were prevalent, resisting change often meant resisting efforts to increase egalitarianism or equality.

The crux of Wilson's theory as stated in the paper is that ambiguity and uncertainty are highly threatening to conservatives. Wilson and his colleagues examined the artistic preferences of people who scored high and those who scored low on the C-Scale (a conservatism-measuring scale he and John Patterson developed in the early 1970s) by soliciting ratings of paintings that had been classified as either simple or complex and either abstract or representational. They found that conservatives exhibited a relatively strong preference for simple rather than complex paintings, with a corresponding but much weaker preference for representational rather than abstract paintings. It was also shown that conservatives were more likely to prefer simple poems over complex poems and unambiguous over ambiguous literary texts. And then, conservatives were more likely than others to favor familiar over unfamiliar music. (I'll have to admit, perhaps a little uneasily, many of the above conservative preferences would apply pretty well to this mostly liberal writer, just saying.)

When the results showing that political conservatives are less tolerant of ambiguity, less open to new experiences, and more avoidant of uncertainty were compared with the attitudes of moderates and liberals, it was speculated that this might explain in a psychological context why congressional Republicans and other prominent conservatives in the United States have repeatedly sought to eliminate public funding for the contemporary arts. Earlier researchers found that authoritarianism was associated with an unwillingness to change work habits and a rejection of new technology. In an East German context of relative interest in work innovation, they found that conservatives were especially likely to value job security over task variety at work.

To round out this major study, it would seem appropriate, in light of what some may consider are somewhat negative attributions given above, to include an initial, more forgiving assumption by the authors. This is that although conservatism—like virtually all other belief systems—in part satisfies some psychological needs, this doesn't mean that conservatism is pathological or its beliefs are necessarily false, irrational, or unprincipled. (Perhaps they mean by that to be related to their core conservative dimension of acceptance of inequality, which, though described in the paper as being a historical view of conservatism, perhaps is acknowledging most peoples' feelings today that this is a negative dimension? The context given is that prior researchers had found it an established principle that the left favors equality "while the right sees society as inevitably hierarchical.") They posit further that most human beliefs are subjectively rational in that though they result from a set of subscribed premises they are also at least partially responsive to reality constraints. (In the case of conservatives and the environment, let us say from their lips to God's ear.)

In one last bit on the lighter side that was found in the article, George F. Will once joked that his "gloomy temperament received its conservative warp from early and prolonged exposure to the Chicago Cubs," a baseball team that has not won the pennant since 1945. Pessimism, he argued, is an essential characteristic of the conservative temperament: "Conservatives know the world is a dark and forbidding place where most new knowledge is false, most improvements are for the worse."

A study by Oxley et al.[24] found that variations in political attitudes correlate with physiological traits. The authors note that the nature and source of political attitudes have been traditionally believed to be built from sensible and straightforward reactions to environmental events, but that more recent research emphasizes the built-in, almost "automated" quality of many political responses. This has been suggested to be based in brain activation variations in limbic regions. They note that broad, physiologically relevant traits such as feelings of disgust and fear of disease have been suggested to be related to political attitudes, and that political beliefs can be predicted by observing brain activation patterns in response to unanticipated events, such as one letter of the alphabet appearing on a computer screen when the respondent expected a different letter.

The study used the physiology of response to a perceived threat for their investigation because they felt an appropriate response to physical threat is necessary for long-term survival and because a perceived threat produces a variety of reasonably well-mapped, physiological responses. If the threat is abrupt, a defensive cascade of linked, rapid actions occurs throughout the body within thirty to fifty milliseconds, presumably to reduce vital-organ vulnerability (e.g., eye blink and retraction of the head). Less immediately, a perceived threat causes signals from the sensory cortex to be relayed to the thalamus and ultimately to the brain stem, resulting in heightened adrenalin-related activity. Acetylcholine, acting primarily through the amygdala, stimulates the release of epinephrine, which in turn leads to the activation of the autonomic nervous system (including sweating and blinking). Though these basic response patterns apply in all people, individual sensitivity to a perceived threat varies widely, making this an attractive investigative method.

A random telephone sample of the population of Lincoln, Nebraska, was screened to identify those with strong political attitudes, regardless of the content of those attitudes. During the first session, the resulting forty-six participants completed a survey ascertaining their political beliefs, personality traits, and demographic characteristics. The survey asked respondents their views (agree, disagree, not sure) toward twenty-eight individual political concepts in a scale or measure of conservative political thought, the Wilson-Patterson conservatism format (first mentioned in the Jost et al. study above). During the second session, about two months after the first, participants were attached to physiological equipment, making it possible to measure skin conductance and startle blink electromyogram (EMG) response. Skin conductance has been closely linked with the psychological concepts of emotion, arousal, and attention and provides relatively direct and undiluted representation of sympathetic activity. Each participant was shown three separate threatening images (a very large spider on the face of a frightened person, a dazed individual with a bloody face, and an open wound with maggots in it) interspersed among a sequence of thirty-three images. The other physiological measure was a startle blink response, which is an involuntary response to a startling noise. Harder blinks (higher blink amplitudes) are indicative of a heightened "fear state." The threatening stimulus was a loud, standardized level of white noise heard by participants through headphones at seven unexpected moments while they were looking at a computer screen containing nothing but a focus point. (sounds like a wonderful time had by all)

They theorized that the degree to which individuals are physiologically responsive to threat appears to indicate the degree to which they advocate policies that protect the existing social structure from both external and internal threats. In this study of adults with strong political beliefs, individuals with measurably lower physical sensitivities to sudden noises and threatening visual images were more likely to support foreign aid, liberal immigration policies, pacifism, and gun control, whereas individuals displaying measurably higher physiological reactions to those same stimuli were more likely to favor defense spending, capital punishment, patriotism, and the Iraq War. They also identified particular positions on eighteen of the twenty-eight original Wilson-Patterson format items as policy issues most likely to be held by individuals particularly concerned about protecting the interests of their group, defined as the United States in mid 2007, from threats. These positions are support for military spending, warrantless searches, the death penalty, the Patriot Act, obedience, patriotism, the Iraq War, school prayer, and Biblical truth; and opposition to pacifism, immigration, gun control, foreign aid, compromise, premarital sex, gay marriage, abortion rights, and pornography.

The conclusion of Oxley et al. is that political attitudes and varying physiological responses to threat may both derive from neural activity patterns surrounding the amygdala, and that there is a connection between localized activation of the amygdala and aversive startle response. They say, given that political and social attitudes are heritable, and since amygdala activity also has been traced to genetics, genetic variation relevant to amygdala activity could affect both physiological responses to threat and political attitudes bearing on threats to the social order.

Two other studies demonstrate the heritability and genetics of political leanings in a broad sense. A study that was done to compare the strength of partisan political leanings in identical twins[25] (who share all of their genes) with that in non-identical twins (who share only half), found that heritability accounts for almost half of the variance. The authors say this suggests we should pay closer attention to the role of biology in the expression of important political behaviors. Another study used quantitative genetic models[26] to examine the sources and intensity of identification with political parties, and found that though genes exert little influence on party identification, genes do appear to mediate the strength of an individual's party identification.

These genetics-based findings add to those cited in more detail in the chapter above regarding the biological evolutionary aspects of neuronal functional structures, epigenetic and neuropeptide systems, and even sub-cellular regulation. Given the evolutionary linkages found here in regard to political identification, the case is now quite strong for an evolutionary basis, as proposed, of our ancestral behavioral strategies to have directly evolved into our modern political philosophies. These studies are consistent with the evolution-based thesis here that conservatives are held strongly to their philosophy through hard-wired behavioral-emotional neural connections. These connections are genetically based, heritable, and sufficiently strong to be discernible through psychological and physiological indicators.

We now shift our focus from the above studies linking political philosophies with several social and physiological drivers, to the psychological linkages between political philosophies, cooperative or competitive tendencies, and feelings about the environment. We must first acknowledge that although there are many variations of both liberal and conservative philosophies, these studies have shown that there are also quite consistent and strongly marked fundamental principles that define them. Besides the definitions for conservatives given in the above studies, dictionary definitions for liberalism and conservatism are restrictive and narrow and often require further definition for some terms used. The *American Heritage Dictionary* defines liberal political views as those "... that favor civil liberties, democratic reforms, and the use of governmental power to promote social progress."

With its imperfections, Wikipedia (2008) had one of the more extensive descriptions of these terms, as well as reflecting probably the broadest public consensus on them. Regarding economic issues, it stated: "Liberals agree that a high quality of health care and education should be available for all citizens," and "… liberals favor special protection for the handicapped, the sick, the disabled, and the aged." Regarding the environment, liberals "… seek to minimize the damage done by the human species on the natural world, and to maximize the regeneration of damaged areas." The above descriptions strongly relate liberal politics with altruistic (cooperative) tendencies, and regarding the environment, liberal politics shows a high concern for and protection of natural resources. Individuals exhibiting cooperative strategies, as described by Axelrod and others, would look to benefit not just themselves but also at least one other, if not the group as a whole. The studies above by Jost et al. and Oxley et al., in terms of supporting social equality, etc., also weigh heavily here. The consistencies between liberal philosophy, cooperative tendencies, and environmental concern are quite clear and beyond reasonable question.

The dictionary definition of conservatism is equally restrictive and narrow: "The disposition in politics to maintain the existing order and to resist or oppose change." What does this mean regarding the environment? Wikipedia stated, "Conservatism in the United States comprises a constellation of political ideologies including fiscal conservatism … as well as support for a strong military, small government and states' rights." As a political description of modern economic conservatism, there is little relevant illustrative definition for our needs, but rather a reference to "right wing politics." In that category, it offers the following: "The right wing tends to believe in social equity rather than social equality. It regards most social inequality as the result of ineradicable natural inequalities, and sees attempts to enforce social equality as utopian or authoritarian (reminiscent of Jost, et al.) Conservatives strongly support the right of property." There was no category for the environment under "conservatism" or "right wing politics" in Wikipedia.

A reasonable summary from this and the studies discussed above regarding conservatism is that people should generally look to care for themselves and not rely on government for help. Regarding the environment, conservatives place primary value on property rights, freedom in economic affairs, and small government, which all relate to little appetite for environmental regulation that might raise anxiety about system instability (from Jost et al. above, and meaning the existing socioeconomic system) and that might threaten or diminish the other values above. The first chapter demonstrated clearly that conservatives (as compared with liberals) have relatively little concern for the environment, according to their legislative voting record and other sources cited earlier. The property-rights issue alone has been used by conservative groups, with much visibility, as a tool to fight further protection of natural resources. Freedom in economic affairs and small government are joint aspects of conservative philosophy that would minimize restrictions on business and industry, and instead restrict government from stepping in with coercive environmental policies. This is unarguable.

We have not studied competition or competitive strategies in this book to the degree that we have studied cooperation, mainly because competition is a much better and widely understood behavior, especially in an intuitive sense with regards to evolution and survival of the fittest. There are obviously many variations of competitive behavior or response, and some were discussed earlier, but for our purposes here, what is intuited is pretty much on the mark. A competitive behavioral strategy would strive to benefit the individual first and foremost (with very little cooperative or altruistic tendencies), with relatively less concern for consequences to externalities such as strangers (nonfamily or group) or by the indicators given above, the environment. The consistency between conservatism, competitive strategies, and relative uncon-cern for the environment should be clear and beyond question.

The relationships discussed above are obviously crucial ele-ments in the theory proposed in this book. There were no scientific references found in the literature for the specific linkages between liberal/cooperative and conservative/competitive characteristics, other than perhaps broad inferences from some of the above-men-tioned studies. The fact that such links have not apparently been previously studied can obviously not be an indictment; there has to be a first for everything. Perhaps a social or behavioral scientist will pick up on this and devise an appropriate test, but that is for the future, and the author believes the science and logic of the link-ages proposed here are fundamentally beyond reproach. For crit-ics of this suggested set of interrelationships, please either provide direct and specific fault with them or (preferably, and) explain any alternative reasoning that would in any way obviate them.

One additional piece of evidence for the theory relies more on a biological/philosophical bent. If indeed the two politi-cal philosophies are the result of direct evolutionary processes, building on the two ancestral behavioral mechanisms, it would be expected that there would be only two and not more. With-out imparting too much weight to the coincidence of similarities between a pair of ancestral traits and a later pair of behavioral/ political characteristics, it might nevertheless not have been pre-dicted that chance alone would have come up with exactly two varieties for both of them. An interesting consideration here is a work by the Swiss philosopher, natural scientist, and developmen-tal theorist Jean Piaget. In his elaborate bio-philosophical book *Adaptation and Intelligence*[27], he proposed that the possibility of many different kinds of behaviors for some traits can shorten the odds of chance occurrence and natural selection, mainstays of Darwinian evolution.

For example, in nature there are relatively minimal basic requirements for the construction of things like bird's nests or spider webs, yet nature has found many different ways for animals to do these things, even in sometimes closely related species. Piaget believed that nature in a sense facilitates the evolution of successful strategies by generating a large variety in the first place, thereby perhaps giving better odds for chance occurrence to play out winners. There are many different kinds of nests and webs, though they are all based on certain characteristics and properties, like strength to withstand natural forces, ability to snare insects, etc. Why then are there only two prevailing basic human political philosophies, liberal and conservative, and two primal behavioral mechanisms, cooperation and competition? A logical explanation is that the former evolved in direct lineage from the preexisting behavioral mechanisms in the process of our human biological and cultural evolution.

In his academic textbook on environmental politics, John Dryzek[28] dissects what he considers the major divisions of human politics relating to the environment. These are all in relation to the reigning "discourse" of our society, "industrialism", which is defined as the "overarching commitment to growth in the quantity of goods and services produced and to the material well-being which that growth brings." Within industrialism are divisions including what he terms "Promethean" (in Greek mythology Prometheus stole fire from Zeus), which is basically the belief that humans have unlimited ability through technology to overcome any problems, including environmental ones. (This view thereby gives those holding it a rationale for despoiling natural resources, since these can be "fixed" or otherwise dealt with.) On the other side, there are various divisions relating to concepts more sensitive to the environment, which recognize that there are limited resources on the earth that need to be protected or conserved.

These divisions are finely divided into segments of environmental political philosophy that are precisely defined, including survivalism, administrative rationalism, democratic pragmatism, economic rationalism, sustainable development, ecological modernization, and green radicalism, itself divided into green romanticism and green rationalism (whew!). In conclusion, Dryzek rejects Promethean ideas out of hand in his belief that an intelligent approach in environmental affairs can be attained, and that it can be developed from aspects of the "green" philosophies above. He calls this synthesis ecological democracy, and believes this concept, which he describes as blurring the boundary between social and natural systems, can be grown through networks, not institutions such as governments. He believes this is now happening widely in the way that environmental issues have generally increased in prominence among popular issues of concern. I'm not so sure. He published his book in the late 1990's, and perhaps there was the fading glimmer of that possibility still present at that time. For the more recent past, as discussed in the introduction and will be more so in the final chapter, where economic weakness has seemed to lower the public's concern for the environment, and for the immediate future, things might not be looking so good. Conservatism might just have the edge when their main argument, the red flag of economic hardship that they run up on any talk of increased regulation, gets more second looks because the economy already is faltering.

CHAPTER 5

Locking It Up

It's now time to lock it up, summarize the evidence, logic, and meaning of the theory of this book, since there has been much information given from different areas that might have left the reader wishing for a chance to recoup and integrate. The main theory, to reiterate, is that our two major opposing political philosophies (liberalism and conservatism) have evolved directly from and in correspondence with our two major primal behavioral response mechanisms (cooperation and competition) in an evolutionarily logical progression, and thus are very tightly ingrained in (some of) us with respect to our individual political philosophies. These philosophies or political beliefs are so strongly held in some of us that they are unlikely to be modified, even in the face of strong countervailing evidence, since they are bound within our emotional, neurobehavioral primal mechanisms. A crucial aspect of the theory is that one side of these belief systems (conservatism) has held sufficient political sway, at least in the United States, to block substantial environmental progress from occurring.

There was first an explanation and description of cooperation theory, and why it has been at least as successful an evolutionary strategy as competition. Though both strategies often work together in the evolutionary development of some species, and competition is commonly thought of as the dominant one (as in survival of the fittest), it turns out that cooperative strategies can often be more effective. Game theory, studies on early human cultural development, and other examples are given that demonstrate this.

(This brings one to wonder how things may have turned out differently if we had evolved cooperation strategies to a more significant degree; whether it may have better ensured our continued survival in the degraded environmental circumstances we now find ourselves in on this planet. A furtherance of this kind of speculation is found in the concluding chapter.)

To summarize other main parts of the theory, we have demonstrated that:

1. Conservatives have always (at least in modern times) obstructed environmental regulation and will likely continue to do so;
2. Our two major primal neurobehavioral pathways have evolved into systems that now encompass our two main political philosophies (in individually varying degrees);
3. These political philosophies are thus in some individuals very strongly held, being deeply ingrained in their genetic neurobehavioral systems, and;
4. The political influence of those with strongly held *conservative* philosophies (rounding back to point 1.) has made it difficult to effectively address the deteriorating environmental conditions on the planet.

Chapter 1 gave considerable detail on point 1. The evidence and cases presented demonstrated that conservatives have consistently obstructed environmental regulation (some rare exceptions are discussed, and they do not obviate the major point), and in large part they don't deny it themselves, based on what they believe are good reasons.

On point 2, Chapter 3 provides scientific evidence for the evolutionary aspects of the theory. The unexpectedly large numbers of mutations that occurred during the rapid evolution of the human brain over a relatively short geologic time points to the likelihood that all those adaptations took hold through the most efficient process, which is onto existing neural networks with the pre-existing function. Though there were many different "natures" that evolved for different species, all neurobehavioral information is transmitted and integrated within conserved primary sensory pathways. Neurotransmitter activities can result in the functional reorganization of neuronal networks, and some forms have been strongly conserved (their existence today can be traced through to ancestral forms).

Regarding point 3, Chapter 4 discussed the work of social scientists, including a recent study of how liberalism and conservatism are associated with psychological and physiological variables, and finding that variations in political attitudes correlate with certain physiological traits. These are important findings because physiological traits are concrete products of genetic systems, and being able to link them to political philosophies means that the latter must also be founded in genes, the evolutionary information packets we receive from our ancestors. The upshot here is that political behaviors evolved (as also demonstrated by the evolution biology work above) within the neurobehavioral complexes in our brains, and obviously did so from more primal forms of those neural mechanisms and networks.

All these studies demonstrate that our cultural evolution occurred very conservatively, building upon existing neural mechanisms, and thus retaining much of the previous aspects of those mechanisms. There is no reasonable alternative. This strong grounding of existing political behavior, locked in through our evolutionary and cultural development, with the demonstrated linked tendencies of liberal/cooperative/pro-environment and conservative/competitive/relative unconcern for the environment, provides a sound basis for;

Point 4, which is that the political "behavior" of conservatism will unceasingly resist any significant tightening of environmental regulation.

A major point here is that when these characteristics are exhibited strongly, in either the conservative or liberal side, they are unlikely to be changed, based on their deep organic and cultural origin. The views will be held even in the face of sometimes strong, logical evidence that may be convincing for most other people. This was discussed as a problem regarding mainly one issue on one side of the two major political fields of thought, conservatism as it applies to the environment (and to some degree associated economic issues). Liberals may have their own egalitarian, some might say utopian, views regarding social issues, including the environment, but they are not the problem in this regard. In fact, a characteristic of liberal thinking is the desire for more responsible environmental controls.

Conservatives who hold their views quite strongly due to deeply ingrained neuropsychological tendencies will hold those views even in the face of obvious evidence that they are wrong, and will grasp at any "evidence" that would support their worldview. Such persons may never think to question a physicist on matters of nuclear physics, or even in most cases a doctor on medical science, but somehow they feel competent to overrule leading scientists in the field of environmental science. Obviously, the first two may never challenge a conservative's worldview, while the environmental scientist often does (not only in global climate change but also, going back further, in air and water pollution, where historical laws and regulations were challenged by industry and political conservatives at every step.)

It was noted in the introduction that the intention here is not to justify the existence of man-made global climate change, but it has to be stated that the summer of 2012 experienced the hottest July on record in the United States. Droughts and fires have engulfed the Midwest and the western states like never before in people's memory (technically, not since the 1950s, which is not so long ago that climate change couldn't have begun taking effect). Hurricanes have been more frequent and of increased intensity in the last decade or so. We have just recently experienced some of the warmest consecutive winters on record in the United States. Anyone who gardens or observes animal behavior and movements in the most general way has clearly seen the direct evidence of climate change, in much different plant blooming times, different animal migration times and patterns, etc. A cynic might say that people who see or hear these strong indicators (besides that scientists have been voicing their alarm for years) but don't believe they're related to climate change must be blindly hypocritical and unthinking (and there may be some aspect of truth to it), but the real factors here are the underlying inherited philosophical views that so strongly influence (and bind) the thoughts and behaviors of conservatives.

It is a reasonable assumption that if political conservatism (as one of at least two existing major political philosophies) tends to block the regulatory reform necessary for ensuring the sustainability of our species on the planet, that philosophy might well be considered evolutionarily maladaptive. Could the evolution of conservatism be an evolutionary "mistake" that would (in sufficient time) be selected out and eventually reduced to the status of a recessive trait, or even eliminated entirely from our philosophical gene pool? Evolutionary scientists Burnham and Johnson[29] said:

"Behavioral mechanisms are not perfect, always optimal, goal seeking devices, but rather context-specific physiological systems that respond to environmental cues in order to engage what was, on average over the course of evolutionary history, the appropriate action. When those cues convey information out of context, then proximate mechanisms will often, unsurprisingly, produce maladaptive and costly behavior."

Lev. 25:23-24. The land is mine and you are but aliens and my tenants. Throughout the country that you hold as a possession, you must provide for the redemption of the land.

CHAPTER 6

Maladaptation, What Maladaptation?

The simplest definition for a maladaptation is a <u>trait</u> (organ, appendage, behavior, color) that is (or has become) more harmful than helpful. It can therefore also signify an adaptation that, while appropriate when established, has become less and less suitable and more of a problem or hindrance in its own right as time goes on. The term maladaptation has actually been previously used in the context of climate change, but mainly about specific policies and practices that can increase vulnerability to climatic circumstances. The circumstances that were described can vary geographically and temporally and can cover a range of sectors, including agriculture, water management, infrastructure, and health. Unfortunately, none of the examples given describe how the maladaptive practices arise (which would be relevant for our purposes here). Starting in the early 1990s, researchers have defined climate change-related maladaptations generally as "practices that do not succeed in reducing vulnerability but instead increase it." This was in fact the definition of a maladaptation in the Third Assessment of the Intergovernmental Panel on Climate Change (IPCC, 2001:990). (It was not continued later in the Fourth Assessment). A maladaptive agricultural practice that has been described in studies in relation to a drought was migration to another area (in which case the migration was a badly advised one).

These kinds of practices can perhaps be termed minor maladaptations, since their practitioners may not have fared well in the case that was studied, but it may have worked for them in the past, or in other groups at different times. It also affects a limited population. In fact other researchers described these examples as simplistic for some of the reasons just given. Scientists at the University of Melbourne[30] wrote about maladaptive actions regarding water management and included a description of the past concept of climate-change maladaptation. These were also, again, limited to specific actions taken in response to a given need. The maladaptation we are talking about here, of course, is much broader, not a practice or even set of practices, but an entire political philosophy or set of sociopolitical views that affect our responses to climate change. If that is the case, then wouldn't an evolved ideological mind-set with the power to block our ability to fight back a global environmental threat rightfully be termed a major maladaptation?

Perhaps calling conservatism a maladaptation is, in light of how it has been used thus far, overly stretching the definition. Even so, it is the best term to use when thinking about the situation we are dealing with here, global climate change. It was shown above that conservatives have had, and will continue to have, a deleterious effect on global climate policy due to the fact that the United States is *the* global superpower (for now at least), and decisions made by conservatives in the US Senate, specifically, have blocked US participation and thus implementation of international treaties on climate change. Perhaps if restricted to those more narrow terms, it might be more in conformance with the prior use. But why artificially limit ourselves just because these past studies of climate-change response did? The fact that conservatism relates directly to how we as a species respond to a threat with the potential to impact how, or even whether, we as humans will survive seems to make it very much an applicable description of a maladaptation.

If maladaptation it is, then what is the proper way to think about the maladapted philosophy of conservatism, and perhaps more importantly, the people who hold these views? On first thought, one might look at the way society normally considers somewhat similar conditions, such as a mutation or congenital deformity or other inherited physical or mental defect. This is with sympathy and attempting to assist people so afflicted. The main difference with regard to those afflicted with conservatism is that the harm is to society, not to the individual. As was noted, conservatives are quite often successful and well-adjusted members of society. Therefore, the same level of sympathy is not appropriate. Nevertheless, as in the above situations, the affliction itself is not totally the individual's fault.

At the same time, there is obviously a range of conservatism, from those who are very conservative in almost all of the characteristics described by psychologists (as in the C-Scale discussed previously), and others who are not as conservative in many areas, or who are very conservative in some areas while less so in others, etc. This relates to the "core" and "peripheral" conservatives in Jost et al. Those with the lesser amount of conviction, or zeal (peripheral) probably would be more amenable to taking into consideration facts or any form of evidence that may counter their initial view in a particular area. Actually, though some more "reasonable" (peripheral) conservatives have already admitted that climate change is probably real, many just can't go quite far enough to admit it may be caused by man. Others, like Republican senator John McCain (even more peripheral, in fact a self-proclaimed maverick) have embraced climate change and allowed that it has human causes. Perhaps public pressure has in some cases already started to turn the course in some degree.

A question that can be asked is what is the appropriate way to think about core conservatives who may have little control over their deeply held convictions when their proposed or real actions would result, for instance, in damage to the environment, compared with peripheral conservatives whose inclinations may be less damaging? Should the opinions of a core conservative who believes strongly that there is no climate change be more deserving of public acceptance because these are after all his core principles? Or should the more moderate, peripheral conservative's views that climate change may be happening but is not man-made be more respected because their convictions seem more reasonable? This may be a question in morality or rhetoric but not one we need to worry about here. Even the question of whether meanness is an issue, regarding the conservative characteristic of acceptance of inequality discussed in the psychological studies, need not be much considered here, except perhaps in whether the quest for profit results in harm to the environment that impacts mainly others, including those of lower economic status (the environmental justice issue).

Nevertheless, conservative convictions are very real and surely are honestly held for the most part. The point being, conservatism is typically strongly held in people who will call themselves conservative. So while we strongly disagree with them on the environment, we have to admit that it is probably to a large degree their deeply held convictions that drive them to hold their anti-environmental views. That being the case, if anger toward them is not justified, preventing them from doing more harm, in whatever legal way possible, certainly is. We'll turn to that in the next and last chapter.

A highly competitive nature has, of course, always been necessary for species "competing" for limited resources such as food, water, mates, etc. Considering that conservatism evolved through our competitive nature, one of the major drives in evolution, it will most likely continue to exist in a portion of the population (it's not going to disappear from our gene pool anytime soon). Conservative (competitive) strategies likely continue to play a role in some aspects of human life, perhaps those associated with career and professional development, economic achievement in the provision of goods and services, sports, and perhaps somewhat in national defense (here especially, though, the strategy of collective/cooperative defense may play a significant role). It's therefore unlikely that an evolutionary selection imperative (i.e., for more cooperation) that is averse to competitive strategies would take place in a time frame that can make a difference in the bleak environmental conditions we are in and heading deeper into.

It may be difficult to tease out whether, when or to what degree competitive aggression outperformed cooperative strategies in what probably evolved as a mixture in the life strategies of many species and their specific behaviors. Many predatory animals probably evoke more a sense of being highly competitive than cooperative in their need to find and kill sufficient prey for their survival and in competition with other predators. However, the highly cooperative pack instincts exhibited by many types of predators are also well-known. Similarly, many herding prey species might be considered to live by mainly a cooperative strategy; however, a highly developed competitive drive is evident also, including among the males of many species in finding and keeping breeding females or in fighting over territory. Of course, this blending has not been completely successful in some animals either, as in the apparent conflicts occurring in behaviors like parental protection. Here often are displayed conflicts between self-preservation and protection of young, as when parent prey animals charge a predator threatening their young but stop short at a crucial distance, where their own survival becomes imperative. It's unlikely that the subtleties of these issues will be definitively worked out, especially when transposing them to complex human behaviors. It's probably safe to say that at least for the foreseeable future it will be impossible to define all aspects of behavior as being driven by mostly competitive/aggressive versus mostly cooperative tendencies.

In linking competitive drives to conservative or Republican politicians, as was noted in the first chapter the link is not absolutely consistent (but it is the greatly predominant relationship). Theodore Roosevelt, a Republican politician at the turn of the last century, didn't seem to be a core conservative, based on his early efforts as mayor of New York City in antitrust actions against big corporations, but he was conservative on other issues. He was certainly one of the greatest conservationists of his time. When Roosevelt became president, the United States had five national parks: Yellowstone, Yosemite, Sequoia, General Grant, and Mount Rainier. Roosevelt doubled the number of national parks to ten. He also added land to Yosemite. In 1902, at his urging, Congress appropriated fifteen thousand dollars for the purchase, feeding, and fencing (for preservation purposes) of buffalo in Yellowstone. Was that the end of conservatism's showing any real regard for conservation? It was noted in Chapter 1 that Republican president Richard Nixon helped establish the Clean Air and

Clean Water Acts, and established the US EPA. Was he acting as a conservation-minded conservative, or was the action merely a sop by a skilled politician to the strong and wide public sentiment against the environmental horror stories that were taking place at the time? Certainly, in the more recent past, there have been few such actions that come to mind of conservatives helping rather than hindering environmental improvement. One that has happened is president G.W. Bush's 2006 designation of the world's largest marine sanctuary in the northern Hawaiian Islands, although there has still yet to be seen what actual restrictions will be associated with it. (Marine sanctuaries have been found to be extraordinarily effective in rejuvenation of fish stocks and other marine life benefits, but those outcomes are very dependent on how the sanctuary is managed; i.e., no fishing, limited fishing, manner of fishing or other uses, etc.)

Nevertheless, competitive drives have obviously been essential in our evolution and if conservatism is linked to these drives as they evolved through our history, it should probably also be assumed to have had evolutionary benefits in our cultural evolution. As mentioned in Jost, et al., it is assumed that many of our past civilizations were hierarchical as opposed to egalitarian, and in those societies an authoritarian or conservative strategy must have been the dominant one (at least among the dominant classes or groups). (It's questionable whether there is any difference in many of today's societies, notwithstanding perhaps the desires of those in charge to maintain appearances to the contrary.) Egalitarian movements were often brutally crushed throughout history. So in many circumstances in our past it might have made more sense (on an evolutionary survival basis at least) for most people to not manifest egalitarian, cooperative drives. The question then is, are competitive drives (and conservatism) still providing evolutionary or cultural benefits in the present time? And if not (as is suggested here in terms of the environment), up to what point in time were they mostly beneficial before becoming mostly detrimental? Some might say that a more cooperative imperative in some of our societies came about upon our technological advancements in nuclear weapons. The Cold War must be assumed to have required some increased level of cooperative behavior, though it was perhaps a somewhat forced and calculating cooperation, and for many people still no doubt a quite fretful one. Still, it is probably the only "war" in history that didn't include the mass killing of people. Others might want to assign the rise of more cooperative behaviors back to when civilizations first built and lived in large cities, which obviously would have required some greater level of cooperative behavior than in the further past, when people mostly lived in scattered villages, or even before that, in ranging bands. (This seems like it might be an interesting research topic for an enterprising graduate student or researcher.)

In Chapter 2, we explored cooperation theory and found that cooperative behaviors could have indeed played an equal if not predominant role in our cultural evolution. If that started to happen as early in our culture as some studies seemed to imply, perhaps the relatively large role popularly portrayed as being the major behavioral factor steering our evolution, our competitive nature, has been overstated. If that is true, and if there was a time or stage when human competitive strategies began to be generally co-opted in some degree (assuming that they were in fact predominant in our early evolution) by more cooperative ones, when might the crossover point have occurred? Most likely it was probably not a point in time for all of the human populations in existence, but more a stage over which the change took place in many of them. We may never know when that stage or transition actually occurred, or whether it occurred to any large extent.

There is the probability of the predominance of conservative behaviors based on the assumed predominance of hierarchical societies in our past, as was mentioned above, but that doesn't rule out a growing cooperative strategy in some aspects of life in those various times and societies. After all, we know that egalitarian-type up-rises occurred at times in the past, perhaps reflecting on the development of classes in our early societies (with ruling classes exhibiting more authoritarian/conservative tendencies while lower classes perhaps exhibiting more cooperative strategies to better enhance their collective survival in their more difficult conditions.) Whatever the actual situations in that sense were in different times in our past, from all that has been presented here it should be clear that now is a time when generally more cooperative and less competitive modes of behavior in our society are imperative. This is not only based on hopefully preventing more killing wars and improvement in social conditions but also regarding the need to deal with decreasing nonrenewable resources like water and other natural resources including fossil fuels, and of course, for the protection of the environment.

An interesting and totally different outcome presents itself if we were to hypothesize a somewhat radically different evolution for ourselves. Since evolution is essentially based on random mutations that have been selected for through exposure to environmental (outside the organism) factors, things could have conceptually turned out totally differently from the situation and conditions we find ourselves in. Even very small differences in the specific characters of our major behavioral mechanisms could have resulted in quite different outcomes. Our early behavioral mechanisms could have evolved to inculcate totally different versions of what are described as competitive and cooperative strategies. For example, the alternate competitive strategies might have included a logic-based concern for the environment that led to devising early, effective and widespread control technologies, and avoiding the environmental damages we see today. Imagine further (it's a stretch, but stick with me a moment) that the correlated alternate cooperative strategies included an altruistic bent so strong and defensive mechanisms so weak such as to diminish the general resolve for providing an adequate defense from organized attackers. Then, those with mostly *cooperative* tendencies (in the form we are conceptualizing) would logically be the behavioral maladaptation. It all depends on the specific adaptations our behavioral mechanisms would have taken on, and what their resulting effects might turn out to be regarding the situations we find ourselves in at a later time.

That is why we need to focus on the reality of what the situation is now. The type of human behavior that is more a competitive one, expressed and exhibited specifically as political conservatism, and with respect to how it affects our ability to adapt to a rapidly changing and deteriorating environment, has become a serious maladaptation in our cultural evolution.

Isaiah 24:4-6. The earth dries up and withers, the world languished and withers, the exalted of the earth languish. The earth lies under its inhabitants; for they have transgressed the laws, violated the statutes, and broken the everlasting covenant. Therefore a curse consumes the earth; its people must bear their guilt.

CHAPTER 7

(Conclusion) Now What?

The above scripture is kind of a downer, and it may overplay our environmental situation a little, but unless things start changing soon it may not be far wrong. It's likely that aspects of both political philosophies will continue to share influence in society for the foreseeable future, barring unexpected eventualities. Is it possible however that we might evolve culturally to a level of cooperation that might allow for sufficiently effective environmental regulation? Burnham and Johnson (referenced previously) said:

"On the contrary, because humans cannot be relied upon to work for the good of the group, we must craft social, economic, environmental and political interactions to ensure cooperation against selfish temptation. Of course, this reality has been one of humankind's most fundamental intellectual and social challenges for centuries, from Plato and Adam Smith, to Marx and the Kyoto conference."

The above thought is somewhat foreboding, and there is no evidence the admonition (or the view associated with it) has proven out in terms of any progress being made. So what hope is there then that a real improvement in direction can happen, and how would it occur? For the first part, the answer unfortunately is, not a whole lot, but you never know. The most likely approaches for improvement are not new but can perhaps be reinvigorated in a different way than has been done until now. The main requirement is that society in general will have to quickly and forthrightly turn toward a greater concern for the environment and drive the opposing views out of major political contention. To help that eventuality along, climate scientists, with other scientists and a broad spectrum of social leaders and organizations strongly supporting them, must be much more vocal and organized in pushing for regulatory reform. This effort should include a new aspect of strongly criticizing (versus only responding to, and often too weakly at that) the self-serving and ill-informed commentary coming from the opposing factions of industrialists, other corporate interests, and conservative politicians and media figures.

What can science and its promoters do to bring the issue more strongly before the public and outmaneuver the opposition? There needs to be a combination of efforts and forces brought to bear, and organized into an effective strategy. All scientists who can in any way participate should be organized through scientific organizations, such as the American Association for the Advancement of Science (AAAS), the National Science Foundation (NSF), Union of Concerned Scientists (UCS), the United Nations' Intergovernmental Panel on Climate Change (IPCC) and any other international, national, regional and local groups. In addition, other potentially environmentally minded associations, other influential sympathetic organizations such as the World Bank (believe it or not, especially now with Dr. Jim Yong

Kim as its president), international unions and organizations, politicians and public personalities and any other influential person or group should be brought in that will, in combination, make up a power base with sufficient resources to make the media and the public stand up and take notice on a sustained basis.

There needs to be a management organization appointed to plan, coordinate and oversee this effort, which by inclusion will necessarily be global in nature. The appointments should follow upon a global outreach by the major environmental groups, US and international, to come together to work toward this broad effort. With such a varied potential group of stakeholders it would be almost impossible, however, to reach consensus on even broad goals, much less specific details. Thus the management organization needs to be first of all, made up of a limited number of representatives, no more than approximately ten. Even this number will not guarantee successful agreement and coordination on all issues, but it will be more likely to do so than will a much larger group. The management group must also be given final decision authority on all matters. In other words, once the group is appointed stakeholder input will be severely limited. This might seem to be a difficult and perhaps counterintuitive goal at these times when wide stakeholder participation has become the prescribed and popular approach in environmental affairs. But if the original organizers and then the appointees have the trust of a sufficient number of stakeholders, it can be done. The overall plan developed then should include a broad statement of goals, an "internal" management plan with specific goals and actions, and a plan for the public at large with also broad goals and some specific and easily understood targets. The internal management plan should have as much specificity as possible, including an organizational structure, an agenda for the effort with tasks and timelines assigned and monitored, and follow-up actions specified.

The plan for public dissemination needn't include specific programmatic details but should include a limited number of talking points, goals and needed actions in dramatic and simple enough terms for the general public to be drawn to and easily grasp.

While the management organization should be of limited number, there should be no dominance by any one group, as this will upset the cooperative nature and perception of the effort by both the participants and the public at large. Specifically, the management group should not be dominated by the IPCC, though that might seem to be appropriate by some due to its present role. The IPCC however, while doing a good job in organizing climate research, has not exactly been inspiring in the public relations arena (more to follow on this). The plan should include identifying and allocating funding for advertising to be placed in major media, including broadcast and cable television, newspapers, magazines, radio, internet, etc., and then nominating spokespersons to get out into these same media sources to get the program out. Part of the media campaign should include outreach and instruction as needed to all weather programs and organizations, whether mainstream television or radio, internet, or any others. These organizations should be challenged directly and with unveiled threat of a consumer boycott if they continue to totally ignore the topic of climate change when discussing relevant large events.

One aspect of the program should be to expose the misinformation that is being pushed out by various vendors. Regarding this, there needs to be adopted a certain winning psychology. This needs to include a frank acceptance of the essential rectitude and honesty of the environmentalist position and the essential faultiness and dishonesty (in many cases) of the opposing side. To grant even minimal credence or respect to any person or group still peddling lies and misinformation about climate change would be, to put it mildly, unfortunate. For those who may believe and use the faulty information from such sources to carry on their own efforts, and thus who may not themselves be technically lying, there should be no deference granted them either, since they are at the least too pathetically incurious to be taken seriously. Therefore, these media and other public appearances by scientists or other spokespersons should not in any way take the form of a debate. A debate signifies that both sides may hold a legitimate truth. The other side doesn't, and there should be no pretense that they do. When a position is supported only by false science and distorted half-truths, both of which result in deception, it is not a position that need be given any respect or allocated any time and energy to respond to. It deserves only the time and effort necessary to expose it with sufficient clarity that its deceitful nature and shameless self servitude become obvious and scorned by even a generally inattentive public.

In fact, the whole point must be to delegitimize these people and groups, inexorably and dispassionately. The opposing forces here are simply incorrect, incorrigible, and harmful, and as noted above, often unable to change their views to boot. In any case, we need not be concerned about saving them from embarrassment, only with saving ourselves and the planet we live on. For that, our spokespersons and all of us indeed must be determined and ruthless in attacking these views and voices of intemperance in our society before it is too late. It's been said many times, "the best defense is a good offense". Environmentalists have been playing defense for too long, and paying the price for it.

Scientists as well as those involved in this effort must learn to utilize the public relations and marketing methods perfected by corporate industry. There is nothing wrong with using the same tools that have long been used by industry to sell us their products and their corporate views. These methods have been proven to work by psychological studies similar to those described above in this book. Why should we let the dark forces of anti-environmentalism keep exclusive use of these tools? Some of these types of approaches have in fact been used by environmental and public-interest groups, and they need to be continued, refined and applied more broadly in a coordinated manner.

And yes, all scientists must support their climate brethren, even if they work in fields not currently being attacked by the corporate lackeys, because their disengagement speaks volumes and their help is sorely needed. Otherwise, climate scientists will continue to be shouted down by the industry gofers and media mavens like Rush Limbaugh and the Fox News crews, and the environment will continue to suffer. Very important also in any sustained effort is that the mainstream media should not be considered as belonging in the "friend" camp. Too often, they present these issues as a legitimate debate, trying to put forth a "balanced" face. What's balanced in giving equal time to people or groups who, at the very least present distorted claims and take a position only because it conveniently coincides with their politics, or for personal or corporate profit? It should not be forgotten that all of the mainstream media have been taken over by a few powerful corporate organizations, and that means all message control is conducted through a policy porthole. Whether that message is really likely to be in the public's interest or in the interests of the corporations who own them, the reader can decide. The media have to be used in this effort of course, but it should always be kept in mind that information given to them can be spun in ways not perhaps intended, and it should therefore always be evaluated for this possibility.

Perhaps not all scientists have the heart to enter the fray, but hiding in their dignified seclusion while Rome burns might not be such a good idea either. The common excuse is that scientists are not necessarily public speakers, and it's not their job to be. Scientists are only fooling themselves, however, if they think they can continue to safely sequester in the sanctuary of their universities and labs, with blinkered focus on their projects and sheltered from the crude give-and-take of the public arena. They may find that their reclusive reticence will instead at some point find them without a project or position if the anti-science sentiment organized by much of industry and its puppets is exacerbated, for example, by a continuing financial and economic downturn.

In a related sense, climate scientists, and probably more so the institutions and journals supporting them have been, in the author's opinion, spending way too much time and resources ensuring their findings are triple and quadruple verified to the point of absurdity, and trying to find effective ways of communicating them to a public that is typically either tuned out or, in the case of conservatives and their supporters, openly hostile to their findings on climate change. Too much hand-wringing and self-flagellation has occurred as a result of recent minor unintended mistakes or overstatements by one or two climatologists, cherry-picked from within a huge body of otherwise overwhelmingly convincing scientific data and findings. These were from e-mails illegally obtained by anti-environmental activists and after a full review by competent international authorities were dismissed as not compromising climate change findings one iota. Yet the self-flagellation continues. To read in science-journal editorials, including in AAAS's *Science*, the repeated navel-gazing, introspective recriminations, and urgent strivings to improve "communication" has sometimes required this writer to put considerable effort into repressing the urge to become physically ill. That placid and staid journal, instead of playing a more useful role in this battle, has apologized too much methinks (although very recent editions have seemed to reflect a slight shift in the right direction). The IPCC, for its part, has also shown an utter lack of will or success in defending its scientists from the opposing forces who have attacked them so viciously. The journals and scientists can't just try to take a moral high ground and explain in erudite terms their complex findings to the often arrogant and unreceptive opposing forces. They also fail to see that if they had the combined communication skills of Bill Clinton, Ronald Reagan, and P.T. Barnum they couldn't convince conservatives of the environmental truth using only their reasoned, measured, and blinkered approach. And trying to stay "above the fray" or restricting themselves to Marquess of Queensberry rules when pitted against a gang of street fighters in televised or radio appearances has only resulted in their getting a serious beat-down in the media.

Maybe that standard approach was alright for when the findings first started coming out, or even for the following five or ten years afterward. The realization hasn't apparently taken hold yet though, that there are powerful forces at work against those findings, or more to the point, against what those findings could bring about if they are allowed to run their course. What the findings can bring to mainly the energy industry and its corporate associates includes at the least, the loss of some control over their business practices, but mainly they can very possibly bring a lesser profit for these mega corporations. Let's be clear that any lesser profit for the powers in control of these industries is still a lesser profit, no matter how much less or what the reasons for it may be. Their talk of the need to watch their bottom lines are mostly about having to provide value for their stockholders. Smaller companies and businesses also have to watch their bottom line, but often their needs are more related to just surviving as a business, or making a satisfactory profit. The kinds of profit we're talking about for the mega oil companies are in the billions, and it probably often relates more to bragging rights with their peers and competitors as much as caring a whole lot about their stockholders. And, yes, it might be interesting to see how many of the CEO's of the mega's like Exxon Mobile and the others are conservatives. If one were to say that this is irrelevant, well, perhaps it isn't. First, it would be foolish to think these people, who are not many in number, don't talk to each other. Of course the collusive practices of the corporate magnates in the early industrial US are well known. Is there much reason to think that a lot has changed over the years for corporate bottom line philosophies, and were it not more regulated today would not those practices still be in place? Also, even if it's only partly true still today that a few people can essentially make policy decisions for an entire industry, now what would you think about how relevant their political philosophy is? What if you were told that the CEO's of all of the five mega oil companies, ExxonMobile, Shell, Chevron, Conoco Phillips and BP America are all conservatives? They in fact all are. If a conservative mindset is baked in, how hard would it be, after all that was presented above, for them to find fault with the global climate change findings, and then decide to fund a campaign to fight them? For something like this we're talking about amounts in the millions, only a tiny percentage of profit. There was recent news and criticism about BP apparently spending more on a PR campaign than what their actual liabilities are in a certain case. It's not at all rare for corporations to spend more on legal or PR fees than what their actual penalties might be. One of the reasons for this is a philosophical one, though with practical overtones. To give in to a socially-administered penalty of any kind connotes onto a corporation a certain lacking in social conscience, something that corporate philosophy requires to be strongly avoided. This also relates to the issue of precedence. If a company can be successfully prosecuted for one kind of environmental infraction, as an example, it can perhaps be more easily prosecuted later for another one. That is why many corporate lawsuits brought by government agencies or private persons end with the company agreeing to pay a fine only under the condition that the judgment does not include any finding of fault. This philosophy applies to any past practices for a corporation or an industry, whether long-running or more recent, or whether for a particular case (i.e., a single product) or for a continuing practice. It includes a high sensitivity to admitting that there is anything wrong with the way things have been done all along, including things like emitting wastes under whatever controls were (or were not) part of its operations, or drilling for oil in deep waters with inadequate controls or contingencies. So, to make a long story not so short (my apologies), there certainly does exist a campaign or set of campaigns set up and funded (obviously not to be found described as such in any corporate income statement) to denigrate, deny, obstruct, and derail the scientific findings on global climate change and its promoters by corporations and industry groups whose bottom lines can potentially be most affected by them.

Scientists, with and through the management organization of an effort as described above should do their best to denounce these self-dealing, junk-science arguments in the strongest terms possible wherever they appear and whenever they get a chance. They must not get caught up though in responding to every scurrilous, nutty, and ignorant claim by the junk-science purveyors and their clan-mates against the valid findings of climate scientists. These can be selectively used, however, and the particularly nutty ones can be used to help expose the stupidity and faultiness of their positions. If climate scientists or even the broader science community tried to do this alone, however, they would not succeed in changing policy in a meaningful way. They might finally get the attention of the public to some degree, but it probably wouldn't last long unless it is part of a sustained program, such as was discussed above.

The effort described above should include a statement, in no uncertain terms, that there is an impending danger, and that there is great confidence that this danger is imminent and in fact proven to be already occurring. The Pentagon, for God's sake, has come out with a report that warns about the probable effects of climate change, including increasing numbers of migrations and refugees due to more regional wars and crop failures, water and food shortages, hurricanes and tornadoes and other catastrophic human and climatic effects! Are conservatives going to put the Pentagon in the same camp with Al Gore? It must be clearly and vigorously stated that the voices of opposition to doing something about this danger are either basically ignorant of the facts or are knowingly obscuring the facts and ignoring or falsifying the evidence because it goes against their economic or philosophical interests.

Those may be strong words, but we are really on the cusp of either still being able to reverse continually worsening environmental effects or not. To not at least try to raise an outcry of the appropriate and commensurate magnitude would be irresponsible. The anti-environmental forces that are at work have been suggested here to be mainly related to those in our society who hold conservative political ideologies. This is not to say, however (and obviously), that all industrialists, or corporatists in general, are conservatives, or even, as stated earlier, that there are no conservatives who have a care for the environment. The position taken here is about the preponderant views of conservatism and actions of conservatives regarding the environment (and to some degree the related economic issues discussed).

The reasons for why economic issues are crucially related to protection of the environment were touched upon briefly earlier.

These include that there are obviously costs associated with not only preventing pollution, such as in development of cleaner technologies and the installation of upgraded emission control equipment, but also in cleaning up toxic areas and other existing pollution. These costs, just as obviously, will or will not be paid and the efforts actually conducted or not depending on the economic and financial conditions of the federal and local governments, the private sector and the economy in general. The economy and the financial conditions of the above sectors will thus dictate whether and to what degree environmental protections or actions will take place. This aspect of public policy is therefore a very relevant issue pertaining to the environment, and given the current economic conditions in this country and globally, and the rapidly deteriorating global climate conditions, it seems appropriate to spend some time looking at these issues a little more closely.

Corporatism, and more broadly capitalism, is practiced by conservatives and liberals, as well as the range of mixtures in between. We will not go too deeply into the economic philosophy of capitalism here as it is related to conservatism or liberalism, other than was discussed above in relation to psychological characteristics of the two political sides on these matters. There have been many cases, nevertheless, when conservatives have tried to paint all liberals as anti-capitalist or even communist. Perhaps those cases can be found, but the fact is most liberals today believe in capitalism. There are many good liberals who are also very successful capitalists, and there are even a few enlightened corporations that seem to have adopted a somewhat more pro-environment corporate philosophy, not only according to the public statements by their CEOs but also by some of their actions. These organizations and corporations should be lauded for their progressive stance (after ensuring, of course, that their positions are for real and not a marketing ploy).

The main difference between how the two political groups view capitalism, however, is key. Liberals believe that capitalism has to be well-regulated, since a totally free market results in excesses and imbalances, with a lot of harm done to middle and lower economic class people who are often the ones most vulnerable. Related to this is the liberal concern for this same group who are left out of the benefits of capitalism even when it appears to be working more or less as it should. So, is this a system that Americans should be proud of, one may ask, when the form of capitalism in place now is working fine for those at or near the top but most other people are struggling? Conservatives usually line up along the free-market side of capitalism, which, as was discussed earlier, is related to their adherence to the principles of maximum individual and economic freedoms and opposition to any regulations that may impinge on them. There is obviously a wide range of views between either political extreme in the general population, and likewise in those involved in capitalist enterprises. The point here is that in most important political decisions that have been made about reducing pollution, corporate enterprises that have an economic stake in those decisions have formed alliances with mainly conservative politicians, who by dint of their free-market philosophies have most strongly and will most likely continue to support and promote corporate interests exclusively, regardless of the associated environmental effects. And the intense pressure brought mainly by political conservatives for deregulation in general has also, in one case, spurred the financial deregulation that led to the international economic collapse that started in 2008, as is discussed further below.

Before we get there though, there is an area of economics in which some conservatives have recently been on the correct side, in the author's opinion, and it might provide for an interesting convergence among some conservatives and liberals, if politics can be put aside for the moment (I know, who is kidding whom?). This is regarding the economic policies associated with and the practices of the US Federal Reserve. This can be a very large subject so we need to kind of stick to the basics here, which include the fact that there are factions of both political groups who correctly blame the Fed for the mistakes made and wrong direction it has been taking for some years now. (The faction that is on the liberal side on this issue is probably smaller than the faction on the conservative side, but let's not get too caught up in details.) Some conservatives might be surprised, and not all liberals would agree (for stupid political loyalty reasons), but there is some convergence on the belief that Fed chairman Ben Bernanke's policy of quantitative easing (QE), which involves excessive and incessant "printing" of money ($85 billion per month in this stage) to buy US Treasuries and (often junky) bank securities. This and his zero interest rate policy (ZIRP) are hurting many more Americans than they are helping. Interest rates are being kept at historically unprecedented low levels for this length of time, and they are seriously hurting retirees by slashing their ability to live in some level of comfort from their savings, as they had planned during much of their lives. Younger savers are being similarly hurt, since their savings in banks and other low-risk vehicles can't keep up with the shamefully understated inflation rate in the past few years and at present. Anyone who believes that the real rate of inflation is as low as the US government portrays it (generally less than 2 percent) hasn't shopped for food, gasoline, health care, or virtually anything else consumers have to buy.

Employment numbers are part of the fraudulent reporting by our government, sorry to say, which uses massaged statistics and inappropriate parameters (like not counting people who have stopped looking for work). This is apparently to try to make people think that the economy is improving, and also, unfortunately, to try to get Americans back into the stock market. The way the latter works is the Fed has been buying Treasuries and all sorts of bonds and other corporate financial paper, like mortgage-backed securities of questionable worthiness (remember those nonperforming junk mortgages?), to the tune of, as mentioned above but bearing re-mention, $85 billion per month. A lot of this money, after going through the primary dealer banks (the large banks that have an ongoing relationship with the Fed to do this), finds its way into the stock market in various ways and has buoyed it back up to the unfounded heights it now enjoys (unless there has been a crash by the time you read this). The Fed actually buys the Treasuries from the primary dealers (who have purchased them directly from the US Treasury under preferential mechanisms) with electronic credit deposits, which the dealer banks can then use to make loans or otherwise invest. Bernanke apparently thinks that if the stock market goes up it will give people confidence to go out and spend and thereby get the real economy to start improving. It hasn't exactly worked, and the Fed is only now starting to rethink the negatives of its policies (like setting up a soaring inflation, hurting savers and retired persons, multiplying its balance sheet and thereby increasing its vulnerability to huge losses and default) and preparing the market for a possibly imminent cut in its financial life line. The stock market has swooned on the days when even a mention of this eventuality was uttered.

Every time the United States releases gross domestic product (GDP) numbers, a primary measure of the growth of the real economy, it adjusts this data for inflation. The reason for this is that if the economy grows at 5 percent but prices also rise at 5 percent, then there really hasn't been any actual growth. A good example is when we were told recently that the quarterly GDP grew at a rate of 0.1 percent. As bad as this number is in terms of a healthy, growing economy, the reality is that if realistic measures of inflation were used, the US economy actually SHRANK at a rate of about -1.0 percent!

The push into the stock market is wrong for small investors, and they must know it because they have not gotten significantly back into the market since the crash of 2008. The pitifully low trading volumes mean that there are just a few big players (i.e., primary dealer banks and their buddies) who are behind the market moves, with no broad public participation. And the public for a change is right. They know the economy isn't growing and the stock market is on perilous, puffed-up terrain, and they can sense there are a lot of potential pitfalls out there. These include the dire financial situation in all of Europe (which can have a large effect on our financial industry and our economy); the looming issues regarding shadow banking (the massive increase to trillions of dollars in financial derivatives, such as credit default swaps); the huge US national debt; and China, which may now be having economic problems after many years of fantastic growth, but which has propped up our economy by buying our national debt in the form of US treasuries. This last one is setting up a situation where we are essentially on mutual assured destruction if those bond prices should fall quickly, as has happened historically before under these conditions. If rates continue to rise and prices fall, as has been happening lately, China will stand to lose hugely in their foreign reserves value, and the US will have increasing difficulty paying the higher interest on our debt, greatly increasing difficulty. This would seem to make one think the two players would want to ensure that any rate increase be gradual and controlled. The unknown, however, is what may any actor do given this delicate balancing and with other related issues beginning to play an increasing role, issues like currency exchanges and the petrodollar (more on this later).

The Fed is trying to scare people out of bonds and back into the market by maintaining super low rates (ZIRP) and showing them a rising stock market (which we all are stupidly missing out on). This strategy helps mainly those either willing to take risky bets on the market (at this point of the inflated market many even pro-market advisors are urging caution) or rich enough to have access to information we all don't get (a recent example is a one-day early leak of Fed minutes to big banks and hedge funds that was freely admitted by the Fed-Oh, sorry!). The Fed strategy hurts retirees and savers, but helps Wall Street and its bankers. The net worth of the top 7% rose since the beginning of the "recovery" in 2008 but declined for the bottom 93%. Median income was lower in 2011 than it was in 1999! The Fed is pleased that assets (stocks) are inflated, and doesn't seem to be much concerned that it is trying to lure the public back into the stock market just when it might be near its top (even though it is very concerned the market will swoon when it stops QE and is feverishly trying to figure out ways to prevent it). People might think the Federal Reserve is a government agency but it was set up as independent from the government, and it is actually funded by and controlled by the big banks that are the primary dealers, including the largest US banks, JP Morgan, Goldman Sachs, Bank of America and Citibank. The president appoints the chairman of the Fed and its 6 member board, but the board members have 14 year terms, so no one president can hope to influence it. Also, the past membership of the board has shown the revolving door policy between government and banks to be very much in place, and this applies to the chairman and the membership of the 12 regional banks of the Federal Reserve.

James Rickards is a financial analyst of long and wide-ranging experience who has been an advisor to the Department of Defense (including in financial war games), the US intelligence services and private hedge funds, and has written a book[31] that lays out the major threats to the dollar and to the national and international economic system brought on by the policies of the Fed. These are the same ones mentioned above including uncontrolled banking high risk activities and excesses (derivatives), QE money printing, and the run up of the huge national debt.

Rickards believes the Fed has tragically misread the Panic of 2008 as being a liquidity crisis, as was the case in the Great Depression with the runs on the banks that occurred then. In that situation though, the banks were basically solvent, they just needed to get loans from the government to tide them over the crisis (which the Fed failed to do). In the 2008 crisis many of the banks were essentially insolvent but the Fed (along with the Treasury) threw tons of TARP money at them when they should have instead closed the insolvent ones down. But friends don't let friends go down the financial crapper, and the Bush holdovers from the big banks like Timothy Geithner and Hank Paulson that were in charge of the Treasury made sure the banks were taken care of, in fact very well taken care of. This, along with the banking actions leading up to it was the financial crime of history and no one has gone to jail for it.

Rickards also summarized the conclusions of the Financial Crisis Inquiry Commission created by Congress in 2009 to look into the causes of the 2008 crisis, and which had heard from seven hundred witnesses and examined millions of pages of documents. The commission concluded that regulatory failure was the primary cause of the crisis, and directly blamed the Fed for failure to perform its responsibilities, "The prime example was the Federal Reserve's pivotal failure to stem the flow of toxic mortgages, which it could have done by setting prudent mortgage-lending standards." I believe that period was around the beginning of my strong interest in international economics and finance, but I knew little of such things then (still don't know a hell of a lot now, but considerably more than then). I remember nevertheless being very skeptical about the frantic calls by mainly Secretary Paulson at news conferences bleating about the impending catastrophe we will all face if the large banks and AIG weren't given billions of dollars. It was very weird to find myself on the same side as Ron Paul and other Republican skeptics. Where were the Democrats that should have been up in arms against throwing this much money at large financial institutions instead of helping people who were losing their homes, as was initially promised? Were they all bought off by the rich big boys, as some on the other side were, or were they too stupidly dumbstruck by the aggressive bullying from Paulson and scared off by the staged complexity of the economics? Either way the spectacle was disgusting!

And, does anyone recall hearing about this seminal finding by the commission in the media? The author recalls tracking the media reports on a daily basis during this time, and had never heard of it. Sure, I could have read the actual report when it came out, but didn't, and I'm sure few other people did either. We (stupidly, it turns out) expect to hear from the mainstream media of things like the important conclusions from a major commission looking into such an earth-shaking, and ongoing event. Why was such a finding not proclaimed loudly by the media? One would think this would be a major story. Instead, I do remember hearing, even fairly recently on radio and TV news talk shows, conservative commentators blaming the crisis on the stupid or dishonest home buyers who took out mortgages on homes they couldn't afford, or the government policy of trying to get more people to be homeowners. Funny that the commission report didn't note either of those as primary causes of the crisis. Could it be that conservatives can feel comfortable making these spurious claims because they know that the media and moderate commentators won't correct them with the truth? Could it be that criticism of the Federal Reserve is severely discouraged in the media through the old boy network between the mega banks and other big corporations, including those few that own the media?

If Ron Paul represents only a portion of the Republican Party, and he wants to audit the Fed there are also many other conservatives in general who are critical of the Fed and its policies. Democrats in Congress hesitate to criticize the policies of a Democratic president and his appointed chairman of the Fed (even if he is a carryover from Bush), but many rank-and-file Democrats know these policies are injurious to their constituents. The party should put politics to one side if it can find the gonads and join with some Republicans to audit the US Federal Reserve regarding what is on its balance sheet (including specifics on the 2008 multi-billion dollar TARP bailout), what is the real level of gold reserves, etc., and Congress should expect serious answers to its questions about the effects of its policies. First question, how are their policies helping average Americans? This is a no-brainer, middle-class, bipartisan issue, and there should be no excuse for not being able to work together on this.

So, a reader may ask, if it's stated here that at least one aspect of conservatism related to the economy may be more right than a liberal one, maybe conservatism isn't really a maladaptation after all? First, it must be remembered that the main point with conservatism being a maladaptation is regarding its policies on the environment. These social and economic issues are important and contributory but are not the subject inherent in the main case being made; the environment is, and the alliances between conservatives and corporate/industrial anti-environmentalists have been well established.

The second part of the answer to the above speculation brings us to an interesting political phenomenon, which is how and why are there sectors in both realms of political thought that differ remarkably with the main lines of their respective doctrines, and almost converge with their opposition. In this case the more libertarian sectors of the conservative creed are more distrusting of the Fed and banks in general than are the more common corporate, commerce-oriented sectors. It is mainly the libertarians like Ron Paul that are most up in arms about auditing, or actually even eliminating, the Federal Reserve. The other side of the coin was exemplified above when liberal Democrats essentially go against their mainline code, which is supposedly to protect the average Joe from greedy corporations and banks, but will instead support a president or his appointees even when their policies are in apparent contradiction to it. There are other instances that can be pointed out where Democrats have taken the wrong side of their supposed code for reasons such as the above one, or for other local or regional issues. An example is the Blue Dog Democrats, mainly from southern states, who are not very liberal but actually more like Republicans than even some of the latter are themselves. So we have Blue Dog Democrats and libertarian Republicans, both of which deviate considerably from their main party codes and potentially have converging views on some issues. It is therefore not surprising that there is sometimes convergence on some issues between groups or sectors of the opposing parties. This could perhaps be seen as a positive, in terms of potentially engendering bipartisanship on some important issues, except for two things. In most cases the sectors with potential interparty convergence are not at the power centers of their respective parties, and even if they were they are so distrusting of each other that except perhaps in some very rare or exceptional cases the convergence would not happen.

A fairly recent arrival of a sector that deviates from their party's mainline coda but is certainly influential, if not actually part of their party power center, is the Tea Party. This group in many ways deviates from central party views but has actually in large part been an important driver of Republican national policy. An unfortunate point here that illustrates the rarity of convergence is that although the potential seemed possible at one point, there is virtually no commonality between this group and any Democrat sector, including even the Blue Dogs, who though quite conservative in some respects still believe, for example, in maintaining at least some aspects of the social safety net, which most Tea Partiers basically scorn. The irony though is that early Tea Partiers could have easily converged in views with some sectors in the Democrat party. These were in relation to the views the original Tea Partiers had of being in favor of more liberty for "regular people" and being anti-big bank, corporations, and their crony politicians. These views were actually quite close to the views of the liberal Occupy Wall Street movement, which was for empowering the "99%" (regular people), against big banks, corporations and their political cohorts in government. Unfortunately, the Tea Party movement seemed to have been stealthily co-opted by more corporate-oriented conservative groups soon after they established, as they seemed to turn less against banks and big business and focused more against big government. They have nevertheless given the more mainstream Republicans, who are still more corporate-oriented and generally more moderate, a lot of problems in trying to set national Republican policies more in keeping with the views of most Americans. House Speaker John Boehner has had to bear the brunt of this stress from the Tea Party, and the irony is that Boehner was in fact only a few years ago considered to be to the right of most mainstream Republicans. It has led to the even more rightward direction of the party, against any bipartisanship with the Democrats, and goes to show how far the Republican Party has shifted to the right in the last several years. The problems the Republicans face is illustrated by claims that many races were lost when Republicans were represented by a Tea Party candidate, where a more mainstream conservative Republican could have won. The Republican Party denies it officially, but exit polls demonstrate it fairly clearly in some state elections. Coming back around to the issue of convergence, when you have these tensions in the Republican party and you have liberal apologists for a Democrat president and his cabinet who are out of sync with their main coda, it complicates the possibility of any bipartisanship that might have opened in light of things like opposition to big bank excesses and to our corporate government. Nevertheless, regardless of these difficulties for convergence in seemingly similar viewpoints held by disparate groups, it is easy to see how similarities can sometimes develop among opposing political factions, especially on topics as broad ranging as economics (and why I found myself on the side of Ron Paul regarding the bank bail-outs). This is a phenomenon of human nature, but it doesn't take away from the fact, and unfortunately so, that similar convergences have not and probably won't develop on the environment.

A quick note on environmental accounting will be given here, much less than it ultimately deserves. Liberals believe economists should calculate and apply a sensible accounting of the environmental and human costs of a corporate or industrial activity just as assiduously as their accountants report the costs of business for a corporation or industry to the IRS. Environmental economists have identified a number of parameters and developed a fair set of cost estimates for them, such as the human health costs of air pollution from a power plant or cement plant, or the loss of a wetland or an aquifer, or even the ecologic and recreational loss of an acid-rain-polluted lake. Industry, however, backed by conservative politicians has rebelled against using these real accounting methods so far. This is, of course, closely related to stricter regulation, which would in fact be necessary to implement these requirements. Some environmental laws in place now require an evaluation of these potential costs to society, but these are described in general, narrative terms, not requiring the assignment of specific dollar costs, both direct and indirect ones. Requiring the specific accounting above would mean revising these laws as well as their regulations. It would also put the issue squarely back at the industrial operators in terms that they themselves use to justify their actions. Requiring a fair accounting of these critical costs of industry would greatly change the cost-benefit analysis of their activities in many cases, and would be a real eye-opener for the public where such environmental or human costs are an issue.

Small incremental changes brought about by a slowly evolving, more environmentally concerned global mind-set, as Dryzek believes is happening, will probably not result in changes timely enough to avert significant environmental effects. In fact, it does not appear to be happening much at all but instead seems to be backsliding during this time of post-global financial crisis, as well as judging by the 2011 talks on global climate-change policy in Durban, where essentially no progress was made. The squeakiest wheel gets the grease, and aggressive conservative industrial/political forces and personalities have in many cases subverted attempts to legislate environmental improvements. Can it really be hoped, then, that even at this environmentally crucial time societal movement toward more cooperative behavior regarding the environment will somehow begin to occur on its own?

The BP oil spill in the Gulf of Mexico in 2010 is a discouraging example and is quite telling. One would have expected that since the Exxon Valdez and more recent oil spills, including in the Gulf, the public's concerns for drilling in sensitive areas would have ensured that sufficiently strict regulatory controls would have been put in place. This has obviously not been the case. And then, even under a Democrat president, and a seemingly fairly liberal one at that, BP was sickeningly allowed to soldier on for months with its ineffectual plans to stop the gushing of oil into the Gulf, was not required to use any of the plainly available equipment offered around the world that could have captured much of it, and was instead allowed to keep spewing out vast quantities of harmful dispersants to minimize the visible effects of the oil. The scientific community specifically cautioned against the use of these dispersants in these vast, never-before-used quantities, based on troubling indications from when they were used in the past, and from laboratory testing. Out of sight-out of mind was the obvious game plan, and the Obama administration unbelievably went along with it. Recent findings from a large-scale ecological monitoring study in the Gulf found that the dispersant used by BP, Corexit, apparently impeded the growth of the very microorganisms naturally present in the Gulf that can break down oil!

This environmental crime was allowed to happen, it can only be surmised, because we have come to a point where the financial powers of business and industry have effectively purchased the US political system, Republican and Democrat, lock, stock, and barrel. It doesn't require a very hard look to verify this sad fact. Consider the fact that after the greatest recession (some say depression) since the Great Depression, starting in 2008 and caused by the financial industry, there has still been no financial regulation passed to prevent it from happening again, now five years later.

How can this be? Are there really not enough politicians in Washington DC that would want to protect this country from another financial crisis as has so recently occurred? Of course, none would want this crisis to happen again, no matter their political persuasion. The problem is obvious in this case: the bribes (sorry, political contributions) from the financial industry is too necessary for many of them in funding their reelection campaigns, to the point that the right thing to do is countermanded by what is for them the necessary thing to do. Adding these congressional votes to the ones already on their side from an ideological basis (conservative support for free market liberties) has resulted in congress giving the banks the freedom to continue to engage in their heinous business practices as they see fit. The same can be said about how the major oil companies have resisted the legislative changes proposed many times but never passed to eliminate the outrageous subsidies they get from the government for "exploration" and related bogus activities. This is a tragic situation that the American people have let happen to them and to our political system, which might eventually (hopefully) cause a mass revulsion and backlash.

All this notwithstanding, and in a way similar to the potential conflict raised earlier about political convergences, it doesn't obviate the theory of this book, as some readers might have once again jumped the gun to surmising (perhaps it is only the author doing the jumping, but I would rather not leave any stones unturned). It is still mainly the political division that is stopping environmental reform. The prostitution of our political system is indeed a mega problem, and as was mentioned earlier, there will always be influence from other factors, like campaign funding needs and constituents' myopic regional issues (such as the Midwest states' fear of increased energy costs from sanctions on coal regardless of the environmental costs to downwind states). But when important national environmental legislation is voted on, it almost always goes according to political philosophy of liberal versus conservative, and thus mainly Democrat versus Republican. This was verified earlier by looking at the voting records on key environmental bills, and further by the positions of the relevant think tanks, party campaign platforms, and the statements of key legislators.

Well then, you might ask, doesn't this show that not all politicians are bought? It does seem to be a hard nut, but it can't be known really what is in any person's mind, or what influences are brought to bear on different issues. Perhaps in situations important enough to require a partisan response, or, being more generous, a serious public-interest response, then such will come forth. Perhaps on issues which are genuinely complicated and subject to obfuscation, motives for particular votes may not be easily discernible by the public and legislators may feel more at ease to vote in favor of their large contributors. When an issue is a particularly complex one, or when it can be made more confusing with conflicting factors and confounding data, such as financial legislation can be, it provides a cover for politicians of both stripes to bend to the financial pressures of the big-money players in our economy. These include the too-big-to-fail (or now also to jail, apparently, according to US Attorney General Eric Holder) banks, that can pressure funding-hungry politicians, and few of the latter have been able to resist the siren calls of big money. This is a system that is seriously in need of reform from a national perspective, and almost everyone knows it. But the fact of the matter remains that, in most of the large political environmental issues like climate change, it is still the huge divide between the views of liberals and conservatives that is in fact the crucial underlying factor.

So what if a strong and overwhelming voice does not arise from the public, scientific community and its proponents to drown out the environmentally destructive forces in our society? Then I believe either a change in the public attitude may finally occur after it's too late to change the environmental direction we will no doubt be already deeply set in, or perhaps other societal courses may take root. In both cases, damage to the environment may already have been significant, and it is difficult to tell what the resulting conditions might be.

In the second case, other societal courses taking root, although Dryzek dismisses, I think rightfully for the most part, a Promethean solution in which technological solutions will be developed to clean up the planet, there is perhaps the possibility of one that uses a quite controversial technology. In the foreword of his book *Consilience*[32], E.O. Wilson, one of our most prominent living biologists, describes the obstacles and potentials to achieving real consilience, which is the use of information gained from multiple disciplines to solve a problem (and which is, of course, central to the argument of this book). Near the end of his book, Wilson turns to the issue of environmental problems and policy. Near the end of this book, it is perhaps fitting that an aspect of his views on the potential for future human development be discussed. Wilson actually discusses this just preceding his discourse on the environment, but he doesn't link the two. I will, however, if only for the biological and social interest aspects of it.

Wilson discusses the notion that with the continuing progress on DNA research and its applications in gene therapy and other areas, a different kind of evolution will become increasingly possible and likely, and that is volitional evolution. By this he means that the human race will be ever more able and tempted to direct its own continuing evolution, in a biological and cultural sense. Thanks to advances in genetics and the related fields now occurring and likely to continue, hereditary change will soon depend more on social choice than on natural selection. He states that collective humanity, with full knowledge of its own genes, can in a few decades select a new direction in its evolution and move there quickly. He doesn't specify what particular direction(s) could be resulting, other than the more probable medical gene therapies, and perhaps even some of the more controversial aspects of social directions like improving intelligence, emotions (as in reducing criminal behavior), creative drive, etc.

Perhaps Wilson was right that society will take advantage of our ingenious technology, but not in the way some conservative Prometheans might ruefully hope, with new technologies that will clean up the mess their policies and machinations have helped to create. If hereditary change may soon depend more on social choice than on natural selection, what might be a more logical direction for this choice to take, if the gravity of the environmental situation gets to a critical point, than movement toward what many may feel would be a more cooperative and sustainability-minded population?

This might sound a little "eugenics-like" and scary, and one might wonder how this could happen in a world that is already suspicious of recombinant DNA technology, much less social engineering. We don't really know what the future will bring, considering the huge social and technological changes we have already gone through in the past century. Still, given that if perceptions change so much that this kind of thing would in any way be seriously considered, they probably would have already resulted in broad changes in environmental policy brought about through the voting booth. Still again, it would be difficult to rule anything out, especially if central planning becomes more instituted in our future world, with social and economic despair caused by increasing environmental and population pressures, with food and water scarcities forcing mass human migrations, and other related economic problems perhaps taking hold. It would be in much different circumstances than can be imagined today, but not ones beyond any possible imagination. A movement such as this might perhaps be influenced with positive outcomes or directions that genetic engineering itself might take.

For example, and as discussed by Wilson, widely accepted and appreciated advancements might take place in the areas of medicine, or when a potential for behavioral engineering of a more socially acceptable type (i.e., improvement of pathological or criminal behavior) is identified and developed. One need also only look at how opinions gradually changed on the use of embryonic stem cells. In this case, even some conservatives who were initially opposed came over to the other side. This type of thing usually happens (in a similar way as with the gay rights issue) when there is either a family member or other close person with a disease (or a sexual orientation) that could potentially be cured (accepted, in the case of gays) through the approach or the understanding. Yes, there has been movement toward non-embryonic stem cells because of the sensitivity, mainly from religious fundamentalists, in using embryonic tissue. But if it is shown that embryonic tissue is demonstrably more effective in curing or preventing diseases, there would be a clamor to let it happen more quickly and the religionists be damned. In the summer of 2013 the UK is preparing to allow a new type of in-vitro fertilization[33] to address mitochondrial diseases, using the introduction of new DNA into a human embryo (for the first time, legally at least). Mitochondria are the energy-producing bodies in all cells, and carry their own DNA, which comes mainly from the egg. The mitochondrial diseases occur from mutations in these genes and therefore are passed down to the child from the mother. The new technique transfers nuclear DNA from the potential parents (from the germ cells, not their mitochondria) into a second egg from a donor with healthy mitochondria and from which the nuclear DNA has been removed. The procedure is not yet ready for human trials but Parliament could vote on a final version by next year. Can population genetic engineering be really so far-fetched, especially in a future that cannot be very clearly visualized or after great turmoil has occurred? So, better watch your step conservatives; don't change your ways on the environment and you might find your conservative genes artificially and permanently selected out of future human populations.

More seriously, for a revolutionary political change to happen there might first have to come a broad realization that things have gotten to the point where real environmental damage has been done and things have to change drastically. Mass political movement from such large changes in perception might then develop and sweep over populations, perhaps in other countries besides the United States (although many countries are already more environmentally attuned than the United States). Maybe it would be accompanied by a realization that the people and groups who have been saying there is nothing to worry about have been wrong, or worse, lying. Many people say President Obama, as an individual, has just gone through a process, having apparently realized after much angst from his supporters that his Republican opponents have no desire to compromise and work with him on any legislation (even ones that they previously supported, much less any of his favored ones). Apparently, just prior to and during his reelection campaign, he finally decided that perhaps they really do only desire to replace him, and to not work seriously with him and the Democrats in dealing with national issues. After Republicans stated clearly near the beginning of his first term that their goal for that session was to replace him, without even mentioning any favored legislative direction other than perhaps more tax relief, they continued on that line consistently, voting down almost everything brought by the president or by Democrats in Congress. Then, finally, it seemed, the president appeared to get it and started being more aggressive and critical. Something like this might happen on a broader popular basis, when enough people realize that they are being played for chumps by big corporate industry and its supporters. A lamplight of hope for this eventuality lives in the internet, where common people have almost equal communication distribution powers as only governments and other authorities have previously had. Freedom of the internet must be maintained at all costs, or there will be much less hope for collective movements and action, either for the environment or civil or other rights of the populace.

There might indeed come to be a confluence of circumstances where a tipping point is reached. For example, most literate people know that environmental pollutants can be a source of many ills and diseases, along with heredity and life habits. As the effects of pollutants in causing disease perhaps become more documented and demonstrated, and as other negative effects from a polluted and mismanaged environment become more evident, there may well develop a broad undercurrent of outrage against people or groups who have been most responsible for them. These will be found to be the politicians who have fought against increased environmental regulation, as well as the corporations and organizations that have been responsible for the polluting, and for influencing politicians with their money and power. This realization will not happen overnight, and the powerful have many ways to continue to divert and redirect the public through the media, the entertainment industry, the sports industry, covertly paid commentators, etc.

It may become more difficult, however, for these efforts to keep a lid on what may become an ever-growing body of evidence and awareness of the deteriorating and unhealthy state of the environment. Also perhaps along this line will be outrage over the continuing loss of species and the despoliation of the beauty of our natural areas and parks. Witness the media coverage (for a day or so at least anyway) and public concern when it was reported that our revered Yellowstone National Park was tainted by another Exxon oil spill. When things like that begin to happen more often and a groundswell of concern and outrage develops, a broader effort may well start in seriously looking to prevent any further deterioration.

If Richard Nixon could be brought to the point of establishing the US EPA, the Clean Air and Clean Water Acts, probably due to the outrageously deteriorating conditions in the country at the time (remember the Cuyahoga!), then perhaps the continuing exposure of evidence of a similar nature regarding climate change may finally bring about groundbreaking environmental reform. It has been seen that political independents will typically vote for more environmental protections when they are shown to be necessary, and the conversion of this group on an emotional level could be a tipping point. So, a political tide moving gradually to the left as more evidence builds in support of more protections may be all that is necessary to start the process of bringing on line better environmental regulation. Two questions, however, are, how much more environmental deterioration in the form of climate effects will have to take place, and will it happen with a magnitude sufficient to generate this level of response before becoming essentially irreversible?

Change like this would obviously not happen in a social vacuum. The near future might bring other significant changes in conditions and in the ways Western society, and perhaps others, operate. Many economists feel that the effects and causes of the global financial crisis of 2008 are still with us in 2013, and that it is subject to recurring in an even worse way because the underlying conditions are still there or have actually grown worse. Abrupt and serious events like this can change how people feel about many things politically and socially. In one sense, there might be less concern for the environment due to increased economic pressure brought by a US or global financial crisis. People might be less concerned about the state of their air and water if other social systems, like food and energy distribution, begin to be disrupted.

On the other hand, a financial and economic crisis could bring about massive social unrest, and blame for those failures and their effects on social structures could fall squarely on the same financial and corporate interests and their supporters that are perceived as also being responsible for the growing environmental degradation. Not only would an economic crisis have devastating effects on how people live, it would obviously put even stricter limitations on how much public monies would be available to clean the environment, from EPA's toxic waste site cleanup program (Superfund), to its nationwide municipal programs that help cities and states, to development of cleaner industrial technologies, and other government- or industry-funded environmental efforts.

Some even mainstream economists say that a global financial collapse could be heading our way and it could be worse than the Great Depression (we are already close to the unemployment numbers of that saga if real unemployment today is used). After the Great Depression, the Glass-Steagall Act, which was passed in 1933, required the huge change in the banking industry that securities and related insurance business could not be conducted by firms that offered the public retail services like savings accounts and mortgage loans. The financial industry fought hard against it from the beginning, getting Congress to try eleven times in the next sixty years to repeal it. Finally, on November 4, 1999, a day that will live in infamy, Glass-Steagall was repealed, over the strenuous objections of Democratic senator Byron Dorgan, but with the shameful consent of almost every other member of Congress, Republican and Democrat. It was pushed through mainly by conservative senators but nevertheless with the support of the Democrat administration of President William Jefferson Clinton.

The financial industry had done such a marvelous job of obfuscating the past and lobbying for the repeal as a needed modernization that Congress and a Democrat administration were almost totally bought over into a snowballing tide of support. The fact is that some of the major banks were already doing securities business, and so the repeal was touted as almost a conforming regulation! And since these banks were already making huge profits on this business (how this was allowed while still under Glass-Steagall is another shameful example of political corruption), they were eager to spread the wealth a little in campaign contributions to go along with the lobbying. Long live the almighty dollar! Only eight senators voted against the repeal, with Dorgan noting that this would create banks that would be "too big to fail" and that we would rue this day within ten years. He was right, but it took only nine years for the bloated, bloviating, and finally bankrupt banking industry to bring on the Great Recession of 2008.

It took only nine years for a second crisis to develop from the repeal of a law that had lasted for sixty years after the Great Depression, which had created the demand for the law in the first place. Now, five years after the onset of the second crisis, there is no legislation in place to prevent the next collapse. There is a half-hearted attempt in writing legislation (Dodd-Frank) to curb the worst financial industry abuses, but it is being heavily lobbied by the banking industry, and there is apparently nothing so far seriously addressing the too-big-to-fail bank trap that is still present. If another bank-caused financial crisis occurs in the next year or two, it would be about half the time that it took for the last one to develop. Something would have to give. No one knows what that would be, but it could end up being what some economists have termed a global financial or currency reset, or at least hyper-inflation from the extravagant and blatant money printing by the Fed. That would severely devalue the dollar, and put huge strains on any government and private resources that could be available for many things, including environmental controls.

One thing that is likely, due to the large US national debt and the decreasing portion of global economic output that now marks the United States, is that the dollar may no longer be the global reserve currency (and the basis for petroleum trading) that it now enjoys. Not long ago, it was announced that Australia and China will enable direct currency convertibility. This followed two years of Chinese efforts to internationalize their currency, the yuan, and included bilateral currency agreements between China and Japan, China and Russia, China and Iran, China and Brazil, and also between India and Iran, among others. Also, as reported by Reuters, "France intends to set up a currency swap line with China to make Paris a major offshore yuan trading hub in Europe, competing against London." Previously, the Bank of England had announced a currency swap with the Bank of China. All of these international and linked currency agreements leave out the United States. It isn't hard to figure that a reason for this is the international, but especially Eastern nations', resentment of the arrogance of the large US banks in their underhanded inter-national monetary dealings, and of the recklessly huge money printing by the US Fed, which devalues their huge holdings of US Treasury bonds. The result of all this would be that for the first time in more than two centuries, control of world economics will have shifted from either British, European, or American primacy to Eastern powers (mainly China and Russia). Such a shift and what it would mean cannot even be imagined by most Western people today, including and probably even more so for Americans, given our comparatively shorter span of economic prominence. Just a sampling of the potential effects would be rampant price inflation of imports and the associated restrictions in some supply lines. Add to this the exportation of US production capability and jobs during the last couple of decades and you have the prescription for a serious and prolonged economic downturn.

So, here we would now have a convergence of potential trends and circumstances that might bring a huge change in social direction, which may or may not include a revolutionary turn toward more environmental concern. First is a growing realization and outrage over the environmental degradation that has been allowed to take place, either through greater climate-related impacts being experienced and/or a growing awareness of the level of damage in general. Then there is the potential for a financial and economic crisis that disrupts society perhaps in ways not seen before in our modern society, and causing a general rethink in all matters of public policy.

Of course, this is all hypothetical, and no one knows where we might be ten, twenty, or fifty years from now. Judging from our recent and not so recent history, humans have not always made good choices on the path of our cultural evolution. There are, though, a couple of potential saving graces for our outlook that bear mentioning, even if only in passing since their potential is still quite unsure. One is that there are indications from groups that look at these things that population growth may actually be stabilizing and even decreasing in many areas of the world (save for Africa, apparently). Should this be the case it could reduce pressure on natural resources in many ways, and could seriously change the global outlook from what was previously estimated. The other is a potential for advances in energy production through the renewable sources of wind and solar. Here is where technology and the Promethean outlook might actually have a chance of achieving some improvements in the environment. Ironically (since they have sometimes taken refuge in the Promethean argument), it is conservatives that have been most vocal against the expenditure of government funds to develop these technologies. If ExxonMobil and other large energy companies were serious and would actually spend the serious money required to put an effective private effort together, it might help. But we don't see that happening to any great extent, especially as a percentage of profits. Conservative politicians have instead raked President Obama over the coals for his alternative energy effort failures (Solyndra), giving little credit to the fact that there are always failures among new technology ventures.

Still, hope remains that technological energy advances could bring about real change in this important area. The other possible hope falls back to a sufficient number of people rising up and organizing, especially through an effort such as was described at the beginning of this chapter. Ironically, if the US's place in world affairs continues to shrink in comparison to other nations, that itself might bring about international environmental improvement, through its lessening influence in world affairs making conservative obstructionism less important. As bad as environmental conditions in China, Russia and India might now be in some locations, they are all looking intently at implementing alternative energy and production technologies, as well as improvement in other practices with environmental impacts. They have experienced the negative environmental effects of Western industrial methods and generally wish to avoid further impacts on their populations, who have become increasingly vocal about these issues. They might actually make the environmental gains that have been stymied by conservatism in this country. This will unfortunately add to the US economic decline through lost opportunity costs.

Even more ironically, it's been thought that the diminishment of US industrial production may already have had some environmental benefits through decreased air and water pollution (no industry-no pollution, though this of course wouldn't have been the favored approach to that result). If production is starting to come back to the US as some claim is happening (even if partly due to the questionably beneficial route of lower American wage rates) hopefully it will do so under better regulatory overview than in the past. Also, depending on whether new or improved energy technologies are implemented here first, this may also lead to a better direction in the US. Hopefully, a national or internationally-based movement as was discussed above may actually come to pass. It is a pity, though, that it otherwise seems it may take considerable additional environmental damage to occur for a large-scale environmental movement to begin. Such, apparently, is human nature. It's also perhaps another, though hopefully not ultimate, indication of the power that our inherent behavioral mechanisms still have in the control of our own destiny.

REFERENCES

1. L. Saad, "Conservatives Maintain Edge as Top Ideological Group," Gallop.com, October 26, 2009 http://www.gallup.com/poll/123854/Conservatives-Maintain-Edge-Top-Ideological-Group.aspx

2. L.A. Dugatkin, *The Altruism Equation: Seven Scientists Search for the Origin of Goodness* (Princeton University Press, 2006).

3. R.L. Trivers, "The Evolution of Reciprocal Altruism," *Quarterly Review Biology*, 46 (1) (1971): 35.

4. R. Dawkins, *The Selfish Gene*, (Oxford University Press, 1976).

5. J.L. Sachs and J.J. Bull, "Experimental evolution of conflict mediation between genomes," *Proceedings of the National Academy of Sciences*, 102 (2005): 390–3955.

6. E.D. Levy, C.R. Landry, and S.W. Michnick, "Signaling Through Cooperation," *Science*, 328 (2010): 983–984.

7. R. Axelrod and W.D. Hamilton, "The Evolution of Cooperation," *Science*, 211 (1981): 1390–1396.

8. W.H. Calvin, *A Brief History of the Mind: From Apes to Intellect and Beyond* (Oxford University Press, 2004).

9. R. Leakey and R. Lewin, *Origins Reconsidered: In Search of What Makes Us Human* (Dell Publishing Group Inc., 1992).

10. I. Eshel and L. L. Cavalli-Sforza, "Assortment of Encounters and Evolution of Cooperativeness," *Proceedings of the National Academy Sciences*, Vol. 79 (1982): 1331–1335.

11. R. Boyd, H. Gintis, and S. Bowles, "Coordinated Punishment of Defectors Sustains Cooperation and Can Proliferate When Rare," *Science*, 328 (2010): 617–620.

12. Samuel Bowles, "Group Competition, Reproductive Leveling, and the Evolution of Human Altruism," *Science*, 314 (2006): 1569–1572.

13. Mary Midgley, *Beast and Man: The Roots of Human Nature* (Cornell University Press, 1978).

14. R.W. Byrne and A. Whiten, *Machiavellian Intelligence: Social Expertise and the Evolution of Intellect in Monkeys, Apes, and Humans* (Oxford: Oxford University Press, 1988).

15. I. Morris, *Why the West Rules—For Now: The Patterns of History and What They Reveal About the Future* (Farrar, Straus and Giroux, 2010).

16. G. D. Bittman and B.X. Friedman, "Evolution of brain structures and adaptive behaviors in humans and other animals: Role of polymorphic genetic variations," *Neuroscientist*, doi: 10.1177/107385840000600407, 6 (2000): 241–251.

17. B.T. Lahn et al., "Accelerated evolution of nervous system genes in the origin of h*omo sapiens*," *Cell*, 119 (2004): 1027–1040.

18. G.E. Robinson, R.D. Fernald, and D.F. Clayton, "Genes and Social Behavior," *Science*, 322 (2008): 896–900.

19. M. Ludwig and G. Leng, "Dendritic peptide release and peptide-dependent behaviours," *Nature Reviews Neuroscience*, **7** (2006): 126–136.

20. Z.R. Donaldson and L.J. Young, "Oxytocin, Vasopressin, and the Neurogenetics of Sociality," *Science*, 322 (2008): 900–904.

21. E.D. Levy, C.R. Landry, and S.W. Michnick, "Signaling Through Cooperation," *Science*, 328 (2010), 983–984.

22. L. Cosmides and J. Tooby, "Evolutionary Psychology: A Primer," Center for Evolutionary Psychology, University of California at Santa Barbara.

23. J.T. Jost et al., "Political Conservatism as Motivated Social Cognition," *Psychological Bulletin*, 129 (2003): 339–75.
Wilson, G. D. (1973a). Development and evaluation of the C-Scale. In G. D. Wilson (Ed.), *The psychology of conservatism* (49–69). London: Academic Press.
Will, G. F. (1998). *Bunts.* New York: Scribner.

24. D.R. Oxley et al., "Political Attitudes Vary with Physiological Traits," *Science*, 321 (2008): 1667–1670.

25. J.E. Settle, C.T. Dawes, and J.H. Fowler, "The Heritability of Partisan Attachment," *Political Research Quarterly*, 62 (2009), 601–613.

26. P.K. Hatemi et al., "Is There a 'Party' in Your Genes?" *Political Research Quarterly*, 62 (2009), 584–600.

27. J. Piaget, *Adaptation and Intelligence* (University of Chicago Press, 1980).

28. J.S. Dryzek, *The Politics of the Earth: Environmental Discourses* (New York: Oxford University Press, 1997).

29. T.C. Burnham and D.D.P. Johnson, "The Biological and Evolutionary Logic of Human Cooperation," *Analyze & Kritik*, 27 (2005): 113–135.

30. J. Barnett and S.J. O'Neill, "Maladaptation: Editorial," *Global Environmental Change*, 20 (2010): 211–213.

31. J. Rickards, Currency Wars: *The Making of the Next Global Crisis* (Penguin, 2011)

32. E.O.Wilson, *Consilience: The Unity of Knowledge* (Knopf, 1998)
33. U.K. Government Plans to Allow Mitochondrial Replacement, June 27, 2013 http://news.sciencemag.org/health/2013/06/u.k.-government-plans-allow-mitochondrial-replacement